Current Controversies in Social Work Ethics: Case Examples

Introduction

The heart of social work is problem solving. Heightened ethical consciousness has brought to the forefront a new realm of problem solving for social workers. These value conflicts have always been with us but, increasingly, we have learned to resolve them through systematic analysis and applications of codes of ethics.

The 1996 *NASW Code of Ethics* (adopted by the NASW Delegate Assembly in 1996 and in effect since January 1, 1997) represents expanded coverage of many topics and organizes standards in a framework that informs and guides professional conduct. How to apply the *Code* is still a challenge for many practitioners, however. When one is in the throes of decision making, the problem at hand—which may have consequential outcomes for clients or for one's career—often seems unique, and the inherent competing values posed appear irreconcilable. This handbook of examples of ethics dilemmas and commentaries is a compilation of practitioners' experiences from NASW's Office of Ethics and Adjudication. In addition, examples were provided by the *NASW Code of Ethics* Revision Committee and NASW chapter ethics committees. The commentaries represent the revision committee's, not NASW's, interpretations. The handbook does not address all the *Code* standards; some commentaries would be redundant. Rather, a cross-section of standards is illustrated by examples and interpretive comments to demonstrate how the *Code* may be relevant in diverse situations. The handbook is expected to be revised over time, and you, the reader, will become our primary illustrator.

The purpose of this handbook is to reflect contemporary practice situations, to explore confusions and controversies, to stimulate dialogue among practitioners, and to help the reader recognize that the lonely position in which one finds oneself when in an ethics dilemma is connected to the larger profession. The justification for a course of action can be derived through systematic problem solving and fruitful consultation with others. The *NASW Code of Ethics* often does not address ethics problems on a level of specificity that is truly satisfying to someone in the midst of a conundrum. Neither will this handbook be likely to capture your unique problem situation. Rather, we hope it will expand thinking by presenting actual situations (disguised by altered detail) and discussions of related considerations and implications.

The handbook is organized chronologically by primary *Code* citation. Each example includes at least the primary relevant citation of a standard; in many instances, there are several applicable standards. The initial listing represents the most relevant *Code* standard; the other citations are chronologically ordered and do not represent a ranking of importance or relevance.

Social workers practice within an ever-changing political, social, and economic context that affects our practice and our clients. Social work practice is itself continually evolving. This creates a dynamic context from which ethics dilemmas emerge for social workers and in which ethics problem solving is both a challenge and an important professional goal.

The *NASW Code of Ethics* is both an important guidepost and a tool for social workers to use in ethical decision making. NASW is providing this handbook to help social workers understand the range of situations with ethics implications that they may encounter and to provide some assistance in understanding how to use the *Code* to help with ethical decision making. NASW invites you to become an active participant in the identification of emerging issues and their ethics implications (see the form for the submission of vignettes and commentaries in the back of this handbook).

Appreciation

The *NASW Code of Ethics* Revision Committee worked with noteworthy commitment over a two-year period to develop a new *Code of Ethics* for the social work profession. Now the combined talents of the committee members have been put to the task of preparing this book of illustrations and brief discussions. NASW recognizes them with gratitude and respect for their work. The committee was composed of Frederic Reamer (chairperson), Carol Brill, Jacqueline Glover, Marjorie Hammock, Sister M. Vincentia Joseph, Alfred Murillo, Barbara Varley, and Drayton Vincent.

Staff who assisted the committee were Elizabeth DuMez and Brenda Oredein. Practicum student Maureen McGlone contributed to the development of this handbook.

1. Social Workers' Ethical Responsibilities to Clients

1

A clinical social worker is helping a female client work through residual problems related to sexual abuse by her father many years earlier. The client had been removed from the home for a period, and her father had gone into treatment. The client's father is a third-grade teacher, and the client strongly suspects that he may be molesting children in his class. The client is unwilling to contact the child protective services (CPS) agency or to confront her father. The social worker shares his client's concern about the father's access to children but is uncertain about the client's clear preference to not report her concerns or evidence to CPS and whether he has any responsibility to report.

1.01; 1.02; 1.03a; 1.07c,d,e

Commentary

In this example, the clinical social worker's responsibility to the larger society and his legal obligations to report this potential molestation of children must take precedence over this client's clear preference not to report. The social worker should, however, weigh the strength of the client's evidence. Because the client has been in treatment, she probably has been made aware that the social worker is obligated under law to report the suspicions, and she may be discussing her concerns because she is searching for someone to do the reporting. All clients, including returning clients, need to be informed that confidentiality is limited by state laws mandating the reporting of child physical and sexual abuse. A consent form including this information and other policies should be presented to and discussed with a client at the beginning of service delivery.

2

An undocumented Mexican woman lives in southern California with her husband and two school-age children. Her husband is frequently physically and verbally abusive to her. She cannot drive and has little facility with English. She is completely dependent on her husband for transportation and assistance with English. She loves her husband and wishes he would not abuse her but fears he may abuse the children if she is not at home. Because she feels she has few options, she rarely seeks medical help. A friend insisted she seek help from the local shelter for battered women, and when she went there, she met with a social worker, who is feeling caught between the shelter's philosophy of encouraging women to leave abusive homes and her client's desire to return home. The social worker understands that through occasional stays at the shelter, her client may become more self-determining and assertive and eventually find safe alternatives for herself and her children. The shelter's board of directors is considering a policy that women must leave abusive situations to receive ongoing services.

1.01; 1.02; 1.05; 1.15; 2.06a; 3.09b

Commentary

Surely the social worker's understanding of cultural factors in this situation is essential to inform her work with and understand the behavior of this client. It is her responsibility to help the client identify and clarify her goals and perhaps develop their priority. The social worker may need to develop a long-range strategy that ensures some continuity of service, despite the interruptions. If the shelter can offer counseling services to clients who are not residing in the shelter, she could work with the client toward strengthening her resolve to change factors in her life and toward obtaining help for the husband. The social worker should initiate a legitimate study of clients' real needs in the context of agency resources and guide the policy and program development of the agency accordingly. If there is not a resolution of the conflicting factors, the social worker should explore other community resources that could better serve the client on an ongoing basis.

3

A social worker employed in a county social services department as an eligibility worker has learned that local welfare reforms direct that she report any new children born to current welfare recipients. She fears that this new reporting requirement could prevent children born into welfare families from receiving income supports later in their lives. The worker is aware of the requirement that social workers should comply with the law. However, she is convinced that reporting newborns might preclude future essential services. The social worker also believes that the new regulations will create a new class of citizens (children born to welfare mothers) that might be discriminated against in various ways. She feels caught between complying with the law and ignoring the law to prevent what she views as likely injustice.

1.01; 1.02; 1.07a,b,c; 3.09a,d; 4.02; 6.04a,b,c,d

Commentary

An addition to the 1996 *Code of Ethics* includes a statement on how to think about situations in which social workers feel their ethical obligations conflict with agency policies or relevant laws or regulations. The *Code of Ethics* leaves open the possibility that a social worker may decide that the ethical course of action is not to enforce agency policy or a law or regulation. The *Code of Ethics* states that the social worker must make a responsible effort to resolve the conflict and should seek proper consultation before making a decision. The ethical issue revolves around the commitment to clients and to clients' self-determination and the commitment to protecting client privacy and the confidentiality of information collected versus the responsibility to the employing organization. The *Code of Ethics* also speaks to social workers' responsibility to not allow their employing organizations to interfere with their ethical practice. If the social worker does decide to comply with the law, it would be crucial to work in the political arena to change this law, as it compels the worker to discriminate against a group of clients, which is not ethical practice.

4

A child protective services worker arranged emergency placement for her Native Alaskan client with a white couple. Aware that the Indian Child Welfare Act includes a preference for placement of Native American children in Native American homes, she sought out Native American family members with whom the child could be placed. The only foster home she could locate was that of the child's aunt, who was an active alcoholic and addict and has a neurological disorder that prevents her from driving or being physically active. The client and her temporary foster parents have developed a close relationship in the few months she has been with them. The foster parents enjoy learning about and locating the youngster's favorite food, are involved with potlatches, and ensure that she attends relevant religious celebrations. They want to continue being the girl's foster parents and are hopeful that they can adopt her. The social worker fears that, if placed with her aunt, the client might not get adequate supervision and could, in fact, be at risk.

1.01; 1.05b,c; 4.02

Commentary

Could it be construed that inordinate emphasis on adherence to same-cultural placement would have the effect of discriminating against a foster home that is entirely qualified, even though the foster parents are not of the same ethnicity? In a hierarchy of values, many social workers would give priority to the needs and protection of children. Perhaps the wisest strategy would be to place the child in the sound home that meets the standards of foster care placement but hold out no expectation that the foster parents would ultimately be able to adopt the child. At the same time, referrals for service and rehabilitation for the aunt could have the effect of preparing her to receive the child at a later point in time for a long-term placement. As the parallel situations evolve, the social worker could assess and reassess the circumstances that are optimal for the child.

5

A clinical social worker provided expert testimony in court in conjunction with a suit filed by parents of an adolescent with schizophrenia. The parents alleged negligence and incompetence in the earlier treatment of their child by another psychotherapist. Now the parents have requested that the social worker become the treating therapist for their son. The social worker acknowledges that she probably has more expertise in the field than anyone else in the semirural area. She is concerned that if she does not agree to treat the boy, he might be denied the best service available. However, she is aware that if she does provide treatment, this could be perceived as a conflict of interest, that is, that she profited from her court-appointed role of doing an assessment and providing testimony in court.

1.01; 1.06b,c; 1.16d; 2.05a; 2.06a

Commentary

Dual relationships with clients may occur simultaneously or consecutively. This case presents an example of a consecutive dual relationship in which the social worker's professional involvement in a client's life might shift from one role (expert witness) to another (therapist). Dual and multiple relationships are not unequivocally unethical. Some dual and multiple relationships are unavoidable when, for example, there are encounters or interactions in a small town in the course of everyday life. In these instances, social workers are responsible for setting clear, appropriate, and culturally sensitive boundaries. Other dual and multiple relationships are avoidable, but not necessarily problematic, such as when a social worker and client are both members of the same church or synagogue.

In this case, the social worker is appropriately concerned about the possibility of a conflict of interest resulting from the dual relationship. However, it does not appear that the social worker's role as a therapist for the child reflects a conflict of interest stemming from the social worker's earlier role as an expert witness. The social worker did not terminate the first relationship in a self-serving way to pursue a lucrative relationship with the client, and there is no inherent conflict between the two roles. Yet the prospect of becoming the therapist could be construed as having biased the social worker's testimony in court. Although, in principle, it might be preferable for the social worker to refer the client to another service provider, this may not be a realistic option in their semirural community in light of the boy's unique clinical needs. At a minimum, the social worker should consult with knowledgeable colleagues to explore all reasonable options and to take reasonable steps to ensure against any conflict of interest.

6

A child protective services worker must present recommendations to the court regarding placement for the 10- and 12-year-old daughters of a recently deceased lesbian mother. Since their separation five years ago, the mother's former lesbian partner has paid monthly child support and all medical and dental costs for the girls. She has also maintained positive relationships with the girls and their mother, visiting regularly and taking the children on vacations. She and the mother had an unwritten understanding that the former partner would become the guardian for the children should something happen to the mother. The biological father maintains only occasional contact with the girls and has arranged for a few visits to his mother and sisters. The father and mother were never married. The social worker favors placing the girls with their father because of her religious convictions in which homosexuality is considered immoral.

1.02; 1.01; 1.03c; 1.05b,c; 1.14; 4.02; 4.06a; 5.01b; 6.01

Commentary

Although the children are not of an age to make a final decision regarding with whom they will reside, their preferences still must be sought and weighed. Limitations in their self-determination should not relate to a social worker's preferences for heterosexual environments, a value she may hold as a private individual but which should be distinguished from her professional position. The girls have grown up with lesbian parental figures, and the social worker's competence should encompass an understanding of such. Social justice issues are inherent in the development of a plan for these youngsters and an optimal environment for them. The social worker's recommendation to the judge is likely to be a significant factor in the outcome for the young clients.

7

A school social worker finds it very difficult to develop a relationship of trust with some of the youths she works with. She knows that they do not believe that what they say to her will not be made known to anyone else. Many of the students have learned and discussed the implications of laws that ensure parent access to student records. One of her students recently confided in her that she is pregnant and needs to decide what to do about it. The girl has stated that she feels old enough to make her decisions and does not want her parents to know until she has developed a plan. She has asked for the social worker's help in sorting out her options but has asked that the social worker not write any notes of their discussions.

1.02; 1.07a,b,c,d,e; 1.14; 3.04b,c

Commentary

The social worker is immediately confronted with supporting the client's right to self-determination and to privacy and confidentiality as opposed to limiting self-determination because of actions that pose serious risk and to acting on behalf of clients who lack capacity to make informed decisions. At this time, the client is asking for the social worker's help in considering alternatives before talking to her parents. Should the client refuse to talk with her parents, the social worker may be ethically bound to take action for the compelling reason that the child or the fetus may be at risk. Certainly, it is the social worker's obligation to inform the client of the anticipated breach of her confidentiality, with whom she will share information, for what purpose, and how she will continue to support the client's needs and interests. In addition, the social worker should include timely documentation in the client's record while at the same time protecting the client's privacy by including only pertinent and necessary information.

8

In the course of treatment of a coworker's former client, a social worker learns that the client and her former therapist were sexually involved during the same time that they had engaged in a professional relationship. The client reports that she has not told others in the agency about the relationship. The social worker would like to discuss the issue with her supervisor and the client's former therapist–lover. The client prefers that the social worker not discuss this matter with her former therapist or with supervisory staff at the agency.

1.03a; 1.02; 1.07c,e; 1.09a; 2.05a,c; 2.11a,b,c,d

Commentary

There are major competing values in this example. There is the issue of the client's right to self-determination, the issue of possible unethical behavior by the former therapist, and the issue of the agency's integrity. Another factor is the social worker's competence—based on education and experience—to judge whether the accusation is most probably fact or fantasy. If the social worker believes the story to be factual, she could seek consultation from her professional organization or regulatory board, revealing only minimal information. Unless the client chooses to take action, there is no legitimate action to be taken by the social worker. If the circumstance is ongoing and assessed as detrimental to the client, the social worker may need to define and describe the limits of confidentiality and the necessity for taking some action. If the client had signed an informed consent form that included explanations regarding the exceptions to confidentiality, then the social worker, together with her client, could make a plan how to proceed. The client's right to self-determination and confidentiality must prevail. Moreover, the social worker does not have direct knowledge, that is, evidence, of an ethics infraction as the basis for taking action.

9

A community organizer was hired by a large northeastern city's social services department to develop solutions to the problem of homeless people's deaths from hypothermia. The city adopted one of the suggestions and is collecting all people sleeping on the streets and taking them to shelters if the temperature falls below 32° F. The emergency nature of the situation and the sparse staffing and transportation resources have the effect of making it an involuntary program. A case worker for some of the clients has demanded that clients should be informed of the option and the consequences of not seeking shelter. The social services department believes they are adhering to statutory requirements to protect citizens and prevent deaths. Department representatives argue that a sizable proportion of the homeless people are not competent to make decisions and that in emergency circumstances there is no time nor means for making those assessments.

1.03a,c,d; 1.02; 1.14; 6.04a,b

Commentary

The dilemma centers on the issues of clients' rights to self-determination versus the client's competence to make decisions, plus the issue of informed consent. Interviewing clients in freezing weather regarding the extreme choices of endangering their lives rather than submitting to transport to an environment they may consciously have rejected appears to be an untenable task. The social workers involved should work toward developing an efficient and effective brief intervention to make the alternatives known, to assess the competence of the involuntary client, and to accord those who have the capacity for informed consent their right to choose a course of action. The risks inherent to this client population suggest that tragedies may ensue from both alternatives of allowing people to stay on the streets and in forcing them into shelter. The workers should build in a method for brief recording so that the emergency decision making can be justified, reviewed, and evaluated. Beyond this direct work, the social worker needs to work to expand choices and opportunities for this population.

10

A member of the Navajo Nation sought and received inpatient substance abuse treatment through a regional native hospital. On returning to his small town, he contacted his community mental health center and requested ongoing treatment. His social worker (a Navajo woman) has five other recovering alcoholics on her caseload. She has experience with the use of the talking stick ceremony and sweat lodge as appropriate and powerful forms of treatment for some Indian clients. She suggests to the agency director that the agency should incorporate these types of interventions in treatment plans as appropriate. The director explains that these forms of treatment are not reimbursable, and they are not adequately researched and proven, so they cannot be included in the agency's accepted interventions.

1.05; 1.04b,c; 3.09c; 4.01c; 5.02c; 6.04b,c

Commentary

Ideally, clients will be connected with social workers who are of their culture or who have a thorough understanding of it. A social worker is obligated to work toward cultural competence, particularly as it relates to client groups or classes with whom the social worker engages. The value of rituals, legends, and alternative methods of problem solving and treatment must be interpreted on behalf of clients, or clients must be given the opportunity to explain and be heard. When systems are entrenched, the social worker has an obligation to try to change or enlighten the system. The social worker should be an activist in trying to bring reasonable change that is responsive to clients' needs and an advocate for vulnerable and oppressed groups.

In this instance, the social worker may need to make an incremental plan beginning with her careful; justifiable use of alternative methods, which she documents; followed by teaching and interpreting these approaches to colleagues; and culminated by efforts to gain recognition for their validity, if proven, by the agency authority.

11

A clinical social worker in a remote community trains paraprofessionals to do mental health counseling with members of their Asian, Pacific Islander, and Central American communities. She believes that well-trained paraprofessionals familiar with community members' cultures and languages could broaden mental health services by bringing cultural depth in service to those communities. Months after those she trained began providing services, the state department that licenses her agency adopted new policies prohibiting unlicensed social workers from providing mental health counseling services. A regional department representative reports that he is considering filing a complaint against the social worker for facilitating the unauthorized practice of social work.

1.05; 2.11e; 5.01e; 6.04a

Commentary

If the state regulatory department instituted a new policy, the social services community should have been given advance notice, opportunity to testify, and notification of the implementation date. If a strategy of social and political action on behalf of the legitimate use of paraprofessionals for certain supportive roles failed, the paraprofessional employees should be given sufficient notice and help in transitions to other employment. But social workers need to initiate influence in defining what work is most appropriately done by professionals and what can be accomplished better by indigenous community members whose depth of cultural understanding and sensitivity would optimize the service delivery to certain populations. A social worker has an obligation to defend colleagues who are unjustly charged with unethical conduct; if other social workers are in accord with this social worker's initiative, they should support her.

12

A Latino social worker is a home health care worker for a hospital in rural Arizona. She has just met with a new client, a 75-year-old Latino man, referred by a community mental health center. Although the man speaks some English, he has little facility with it and is unable to describe his symptoms well. His English reading and language skills were limited in his younger years and have continued to diminish with age. The psychiatrist at the community mental health center diagnosed the client as depressed and gave him a prescription for the treatment of depression. The client has explained to the social worker that he was interviewed in English and did not always understand the doctor's questions. She also learned that he does not understand the purpose or regimen for the medication he was given. The social worker reviews his medical and mental health history and speculates that the client may be experiencing dementia, Alzheimer's type.

1.05a,b; 1.03b,c; 2.05

Commentary

Collaboration between the disciplines can be initiated by the social worker. If collaboration has been built over time, the social worker should confer with the psychiatrist to share her opinion about an alternative diagnosis. Although serving as a translator may not be the usual function of a social worker, in an instance in which substantive discussion between a client and two professionals differs markedly, the social worker may have to serve as both an interpreter of culture and an arbiter of conclusions that could profoundly affect the medical treatment and future care of a vulnerable client.

13

A school social worker has enjoyed a good working relationship with staff involved with a private case management company. He has come to know the company while participating in interdisciplinary team meetings facilitated by the company's staff for students and families with whom he works. The chief executive of the firm has invited the social worker to invest in the company as a partner. The social worker has the funds to invest and believes that the company does good work. However, he is not certain that he could continue to work on interdisciplinary teams facilitated by the company and is concerned that if he refers students to the firm's services in the future, this would be construed as a conflict of interest.

1.06a,b

Commentary

The social worker's ethics concern is justified. The *Code of Ethics* states that social workers should be alert to and avoid conflicts of interest that interfere with the exercise of professional discretion and impartial judgment. The *Code* further states that social workers should not take unfair advantage of any professional relationship to further business interests.

14

When a nonprofit hospital downsized, all social work positions were eliminated. The social workers were transferred to an affiliated home health care agency. The hospital then offered to contract with the home health social workers for the same work they had done previously for the hospital. At times, the social workers who do both hospital and home-based work experience conflicts of interest when faced with the need to refer hospital patients to home-based services. The social workers understand that they should not exclusively refer to the hospital's home health care agency and that self-determination requires that patients have information about a range of available, appropriate services. But from the patient's perspective they also see that it would often be more desirable to be able to continue to work with the social worker who had been assigned during the hospitalization period. The hospital's risk management officer has argued, however, that when patients chose their home health care agency the same social worker should not continue to work with a patient because of the appearance of conflict of interest—that is, the social worker would receive compensation for services because of a referral he or she made.

1.06a,b; 1.02; 1.03a; 1.16e,f; 2.06a; 3.09c,d

Commentary

The ethics conflict in this case results from the social workers' wanting to provide continuity of care for clients and the problems of entering into a dual relationship and benefiting from a professional relationship. It is not proper for the hospital administration to limit client access to services to the agency affiliated with the hospital itself; this raises restraint-of-trade issues. Although client self-determination is an issue in this case, the *Code of Ethics* also speaks to social workers being alert to and avoiding conflicts of interest that could interfere with the execution of impartial professional judgment. Social workers must not take unfair advantage of a professional relationship. Prudent social workers should be able to demonstrate that they have fairly offered all appropriate alternatives for ongoing services.

15

A social worker provides counseling with a health and wellness focus. She also has a distributorship for vitamins and other health products. She wants to make these products available to her clients because she feels they are good and useful. She does not believe that selling these products to her clients would exploit her clients, because the only benefit she receives from increased product sales is a decreased product cost (she uses the products herself).

1.06a,c

Commentary

Social workers must be careful to avoid inappropriate dual and multiple relationships with their clients. In this case, a social worker is involved in a separate business enterprise that is only tangentially related to her social work practice. Involving clients in this side business, in principle, could lead to a conflict of interest. Although the social worker may not benefit directly from selling the vitamins and other health products to her clients, the lower product cost resulting from increased sales could provide the social worker with an incentive to promote her product among her clients. Her professional discretion and objective judgment could be compromised and, moreover, she could be perceived as taking unfair advantage of clients to further her business interests. In addition, it is possible that clients who purchase the social worker's products would be dissatisfied with their performance or experience unpleasant or even harmful side effects. As a result, the clients might feel angry, betrayed, or exploited; this certainly could complicate the clinical relationship and, ultimately, have a detrimental effect on the clients' well-being.

16

A child protective services (CPS) client, widowed six months earlier, is unemployed and has a five-year-old daughter for whom she feels incapable of providing good care. After much deliberation, the client has decided that she should relinquish her daughter for adoption. The client observes that her social worker is good with children and enjoys the child. The client also overhears the social worker talking with other staff about her plans to try to adopt a second child. The client then tells the social worker what she has overheard and wonders if she would consider being the adoptive parent for her daughter.

1.06a,c; 1.01

Commentary

This social worker has encountered a potential conflict of interest in her relationship with the client. One form of conflict involves clients' offers of goods or services to social workers apart from the professional–client relationship that would benefit the social worker personally. In this case the client broached the possibility of placing her child with the social worker for adoption. The client may be making a good-faith effort to plan for the best interest of her child.

This kind of dual or multiple relationship could be harmful to the client. Psychodynamically, the client may be trying to please the authority figure, the social worker. The worker could contemplate a justification of "rescuing" a child in whom she may already have an emotional investment. As a CPS worker, the social worker has considerable influence on and control over the client's life. The mere prospect of becoming the adoptive parent of her client's child would certainly alter the dynamics in the professional–client relationship and could interfere with the exercise of professional discretion and impartial judgment. Social workers must not take unfair advantage of any professional relationship or exploit clients to further personal interests and should not engage in dual or multiple relationships with a client. Social workers' primary responsibility is to promote the well-being of their clients, not set up emotional complications. They must not allow their own personal interests to interfere with these fundamental commitments.

17

A rural social worker who provides clinical services at a nursing home has agreed to assume medical power of attorney for a number of patients who have no other appropriate resources. The social worker differentiates the roles, never providing counseling to the patients for whom he has the legally sanctioned role and responsibility. One effect is that clients to whom he provides counseling can never have the opportunity to select him as their legal representative, and clients for whom he has power of attorney cannot receive clinical services.

1.06a,c; 1.02; 1.03a; 1.14

Commentary

Underserved jurisdictions inevitably have the complication of an insufficient range of available services for many clients. The social worker seems to have made a provision to avoid conflict of interest that could possibly have undermined his impartiality in providing service that almost certainly would give that appearance. Who is to say that his availability in one role or the other is more important to a particular client? Clients should have some say in how they want to use the skills of the available social worker. Further, the social worker should endeavor to locate or develop supplemental sources (for example, volunteers who could assume medical power of attorney) to help address the range of needs of his clientele.

18

A social worker who serves as the clinical director for an employee assistance program (EAP) also has a small psychotherapy practice. In the course of his private practice sessions with a client, the social worker is impressed with the client's common sense and humor. He also knows that this client is searching for new employment. The social worker's EAP needs an office manager—the type of work that the client reports enjoying and doing well. The social worker would like to recommend that the client apply for the office manager position at the EAP.

1.06a,c; 6.04b

Commentary

Although social workers are responsible for expanding opportunities for their clients, this specific situation would create a conflict of interest for the social worker and client. The conflicts of appearance of preferential treatment for the client; of the possibility that the client's performance would be, in part, appraised by the social worker; and that the client would be expected to or seen as giving preference to this social worker's support needs all pose serious questions. If the client were hired by the EAP, the social worker and the client would then have a dual relationship. But is there a real risk of exploitation of or potential harm to the client? If the client were to learn independently about the position, it is the social worker's responsibility to inform his client of the potential conflicts, including probable termination of the therapeutic services. The social worker and the client must be guided by the client's needs.

19

A community organizer applies for a personal loan at a bank. One year earlier she had helped a group of tenants obtain funding through the same bank to take ownership of their apartment complex. She is turned down for the loan she sought for not having a long enough work history. The officer who advised her of the bank's decision is an individual with whom she had worked in the tenant ownership effort. The bank officer offers to give her the loan from her personal funds on the same terms the bank would offer.

1.06b

Commentary

The ethics conflict this community organizer faces stems from being offered the opportunity of using a professional relationship for personal gain. Because the community organizer met the bank officer in her professional social work capacity, it might be a conflict of interest to accept the personal loan from the bank officer. The *Code of Ethics* clearly states that social workers should not use their professional relationships to further their own business interests. There is always the potential that if problems develop around this loan it could affect the bank officer's relationship to the community organizer's clients, the tenants in the apartment complex.

20

An independent case manager for senior citizens in a small town recently received notice that her apartment had been sold and she must move. One of her clients owns an apartment complex and has mentioned that there is a vacancy. The social worker is considering transferring the client to a local nonprofit agency that provides case management services similar to hers, thus freeing her to rent the apartment without an appearance of conflict of interest.

1.06b; 1.02; 1.16d; 3.07a

Commentary

A social worker may find that a client has access to a valuable resource; in this instance, the social worker could benefit from the client's ownership of an apartment complex. Although it may be tempting to take advantage of a client's access to such a resource and the client's largess, the social worker must avoid engaging in this kind of dual relationship, in which services are terminated to pursue a business relationship with a client, because of the potential harm (disadvantage) to the client.

There are several possible risks. First, the dynamics in the clinical relationship would likely change in a way that could be detrimental (not optimally in the client's best interest) to the client. The social worker and client would need to relate to each other in the context of a business relationship, which may interfere with the client's ability to take full advantage of the therapeutic relationship. This may result in part because the client would begin to view the social worker as a tenant as well as a counselor; similarly, the social worker would begin to view the client as a landlord as well as a client. Second, the social worker's decision to refer the client to another service provider may not be to the client's advantage. The break in continuity of service could affect the extent to which the client benefits from the services. Moreover, the client may feel some pressure to consent to this arrangement because of the client's dependence on the social worker. Finally, the relationship between the client and social worker could be undermined if the social worker's new apartment is somehow defective or unsatisfactory. Addressing this problem could complicate the social worker–client relationship in a way that is not in the best interests of the client as a client.

21

A clinical social worker attached to a family services agency wants to establish a business jointly with a former client. They propose to market environmentally sensitive products. The social worker believes that marketing these products to her clients would be an adjunct to counseling, because it would enhance the quality of their lives.

1.06b,c; 1.04c

Commentary

It is questionable whether the social worker should engage in a business relationship with a former client because there is potential for exploitation of the client's resources (money) and for placing the client at a psychological disadvantage. In their past relationship, the focus was on the client's needs; a business relationship has a significantly different focus. Such a change also closes the door to further counseling with the social worker. In addition, the social worker should not market these products to her clients, because the products are not accepted adjuncts to social work practice, and clients may not feel free to reject the purchase of them.

22

A social worker is part of a social work group practice that wants to rent space in a doctors' office complex. The social worker has been providing psychotherapy services to the managing physician for the doctors' group that has offered the office space. The physician has not revealed to his colleagues that he is seeking service from the social worker and prefers that this knowledge not be made available to his colleagues.

1.06b,c; 1.07a

Commentary

The prevailing standard in this example is the client's right to privacy and the social worker's obligation to protect the confidentiality of all information gained in the course of her professional service. The interests and needs of the client are paramount. Because the social worker is in a difficult position with the colleagues in the group practice, the social worker should consider whether there are compelling reasons for not renting this particular space and thus revealing that the physician is a client. If the group proceeds with renting this space, the social worker and her client are confronted by a dual relationship and the issues of conflicting interests. If the group rents the office space, the social worker would then be confronted with an ethics dilemma created by a team decision. Ideally, prior group discussions would have established policies and procedures for resolving such potential conflicts. If the individual social worker who provides psychotherapeutic services to the individual physician can remove herself from administrative decision making, she may be able to maintain clear boundaries. Various protective measures would have to be put in place to protect the privacy of the physician–client.

23

During her second-year practicum, an MSW student worked in a small town at a for-profit mental health clinic providing case management services. At the close of her internship, she terminated with all of her clients and advised them she would be leaving the region. The student had grown especially fond of and concerned for one of her clients, who asked that they stay in contact after the student's departure. The student agreed to this request, concluding that casual contact would not represent any conflict of interest or dual relationship—especially because she was leaving the area and had no plans to return. The client wrote occasionally, updating the student on various life events. The student responded with mildly personal updates on her own life. One year later, the social worker accepts a position in the same town where her former client lives. When the client learns that the social worker has returned to the region, the client seeks her out to ask her to resume clinical services.

1.06c

Commentary

Clients sometimes want to stay in touch with social workers following the termination of the professional–client relationship. The client may have in mind relatively infrequent contact, as opposed to entering into an intimate relationship or friendship that entails regular social contact. Social workers must manage this kind of posttermination contact carefully. Some social workers agree to have occasional, informal contact with a client primarily for the client to provide the social worker with an "update." Such contact occurs in the social worker's office, although the contact may not take the form of a formal session for which the social worker expects payment. An example is a former client who goes off to college and, during school vacations, arranges to stop by the social worker's office for a brief chat and update. The social worker talks with the client about the nature of their relationship—especially that it is not a friendship—and that it is important for their contact to occur in a professional context.

Social workers must avoid posttermination contact that takes the form of a dual or multiple relationship in which there is a risk of exploitation or harm to the client, for example, promoting unhealthy dependency or creating confusing boundaries. In general, social workers should not arrange to have posttermination *social* contact with a client and should not enter into a new phase of a relationship in which the social worker discloses personal information that resembles the way a friend shares information with a friend. Such boundaries are particularly important when a possibility exists that the former client may want to resume receiving services from the social worker.

24

A private clinical practitioner whose husband runs a Christian social club enjoys attending many of the club's functions. The club organizes field trips, evenings of games and refreshments, classes, and dances. Some of the club's members know that the club director's wife is a therapist and have asked that she provide services for them, noting that they feel especially comfortable with her because they seem to share similar values and beliefs.

1.06c

Commentary

The *Code of Ethics* states clearly that social workers should not engage in dual or multiple relationships with clients in which there is a risk of potential harm to the client. Although some dual or multiple relationships are unavoidable, this case provides an example of dual relationships that are, indeed, avoidable. The social worker "enjoys attending many of the club's functions." Unless the social worker decides to stop participating in the club's activities, the social worker should not provide professional services to club members. To do so would be to knowingly engage in an avoidable dual or multiple relationship. Such a relationship could be detrimental to club members who see the social worker professionally, because of the blurred boundaries, the stress of relating to her in different ways in different settings, and the legitimate concern that the clients' privacy and confidentiality might be breached, albeit inadvertently. One could expect that club members who become the social worker's clients may have difficulty understanding the nature of their relationship with the social worker, whether it is primarily social or professional. This could undermine the social worker's effectiveness with the club members' efforts to address issues in their lives.

25

A social worker who has been in practice for 20 years has a client with a serious psychiatric problem resulting from trauma and brainwashing. The client left the home where he was boarding because of verbal attacks and other disruptions. The social worker spent many hours locating an emergency placement but was unsuccessful, partially because the crisis occurred over the winter holidays. Ultimately, she "went beyond the call of duty" and housed the client in her own home until he can be admitted for organic and psychiatric evaluation at a prominent mental health facility. She informs the client's family, who are geographically distant, daily of his increasing mental stability. The social worker confers informally with a psychiatrist and another clinical social worker, who have complimented her on her extraordinary dedication. The social worker is being reimbursed by the client's family for expenses incurred in housing him, feeding him, and making arrangements for his ongoing care and treatment.

1.06c; 1.01; 1.14; 6.01

Commentary

The social worker wishes to promote the well-being of the client at the risk of engaging in multiple role relationships. This places the client in a vulnerable position and may jeopardize the therapeutic relationship. The worker has a custodial–caretaker role that involves a financial exchange as well as a therapeutic role. The relationship with the client seems to be productive, and this could be negatively affected through a loss of objectivity and the familiarity that might result in having the client in her home. In addition, there may be a question of the worker's competence to work with his many needs. The facts regarding his leaving the boarding home are not clear. This, as well as his stated condition, raises the question about the safety of the social worker and her responsibility to herself.

Home situations can be stabilized, at least temporarily, and resources negotiated to meet emergencies. Self-awareness is important in such situations, because sometimes one's own needs can get in the way of setting up an effective plan with the client or family. If there is question about the client's capacity to make an informed consent, the involvement of family or a surrogate is needed. One could argue that in a community that lacks resources, multiple relationships cannot be avoided. If this is the case, the social worker may feel that her commitment to the client is supported by the *Code of Ethics*. The social worker, in assuming multiple roles, should be knowledgeable about her professional obligation to set the boundaries of the relationship to ensure that the client is not harmed or exploited.

In keeping with the mission of the profession and the *Code*, the social worker has the responsibility to promote the general welfare of the community. In this case, she and others should examine community needs and work to develop resources to meet emergencies.

26

A social worker who is a specialist in substance abuse treatment has worked for one year with a client whose issues relate to substance abuse and AIDS. The client, who has lost friends to AIDS and has stopped seeing other friends with whom he had previous drug and alcohol use connections, has only one living family member, who is in a treatment center for chemical dependency. He has come to see his social worker as his closest confidant and source of emotional support. The social worker has become appreciative of his time with this client because their discussions have helped him acquire a broader worldview. Once, when the client was too ill to travel, the social worker visited him at his home and then facilitated augmented nursing services for him. The client does not expect to outlive his next serious illness and does not wish to have artificial means used to prolong his life. He wants the social worker to assume medical power of attorney for him, because he feels there is no one in his life whom he can trust to honor his wishes. He also wants the social worker to accept a gift of a pocket watch that had belonged to his favorite grandfather and to be the primary beneficiary in his will.

1.06c; 1.01; 2.05a

Commentary

Clients sometimes hold their social workers in enormously high regard, entrusting them with the most important aspects of their lives. This trust may take the form of sharing deeply personal information with or delegating significant responsibility to social workers. Social workers with such responsibility must be scrupulous in their efforts to place clients' interests above their own and avoid any conflict of interest. For example, the social worker who is requested to assume medical power of attorney should consult with a knowledgeable lawyer about the client's legal options, keeping in mind the social worker's obligation to avoid any conflict of interest. The social worker has an obligation to help ensure that the client's needs and wishes are honored but also that the client has complete information about other sources of help or service.

There are no explicit ethics standards concerning social workers being named in a client's will. As a matter of principle, social workers must avoid any activities that take advantage of a professional relationship to further their own personal interests. Social workers who are named in a client's will should be concerned, at the very least, about the appearance of impropriety. For example, surviving family and friends, who could come forward after a client's death, may raise questions about the social worker's influence on the client. Social workers who find that they have been named in a client's will should consult colleagues and legal counsel to determine the most appropriate way to avoid any conflict of interest and the reality or appearance of impropriety.

27

Two social workers (a man and a woman) who attended the same graduate social work program worked together in the same county government office following graduation. Later, they worked in different agencies but maintained friendly contact. The male social worker called his female colleague and friend to ask her to be his therapist. He explained that he had just discovered that he was HIV positive and felt that his friend and colleague was the only person he could feel safe talking to about his issues. He asked his colleague not to document anything about his HIV status or his sexual experience with other men. He suggested that they identify the presenting problem as "adjustment disorder" so that the insurance company could cover therapy costs.

1.06c; 1.07a; 3.04a,c; 3.05; 4.04

Commentary

The *Code of Ethics* requires that social workers not engage in dual relationships in which there is a risk of potential harm to the client. One could argue that there may be minimal risk of harm in this case. However, because the social workers are friends it would be difficult to establish clear boundaries and maintain objectivity, which could jeopardize effective treatment. On the other hand, if there are few social workers in the geographic area in which the social workers reside, it might be argued that a dual relationship in this case would be justified. If the female therapist agreed to accept the social worker as her client, the responsibility to monitor the relationship and set appropriate boundaries would rest with her. Such relationships create a risk for both parties and should be avoided.

Regarding his request that his HIV status and sexual experience be withheld from the record and that, for insurance purposes, his presenting problem be identified as an adjustment disorder, it would seem that more information about his emotional and physical status would be required. Standards of ethics require accuracy of documentation and that billing practices reflect the nature and extent of the services provided. On the other hand, it is necessary that the client's privacy be protected except in particular circumstances or with forewarning to or consent from the client. Because the client is requesting therapy, there may indeed be issues outside of his medical diagnosis that suggest an alternate diagnosis. It would be advisable for the social worker to seek consultation regarding billing arrangements.

28

A lesbian social worker provided individual psychotherapy services in a small town where lesbians represented a large proportion of her clients. She treated a client for approximately six months and later developed a casual friendship with this client. About two years after the client and social worker terminated their therapeutic relationship, the client committed suicide. Community members knew of the previous therapy history and, after the suicide, questioned the nature of the subsequent relationship between them.

1.06c; 1.07r

Commentary

Social workers must be careful not to develop inappropriate relationships with clients following termination of the professional–client relationship. These can range from sexual relationships to, as in this case, casual friendships. The overriding consideration should be the potential harm that could result from a subsequent nonprofessional relationship. As a general rule, social workers should not engage in a dual or multiple relationship with a former client in which there is a risk of exploitation or of potential harm to the client. Social workers must always keep in mind the possibility that a friendship with a former client could undermine the therapeutic benefits achieved during the course of the professional–client relationship. Issues that arise in the posttermination friendship could lead the former client to feel betrayed or exploited and could lead to the appearance of impropriety. The requirements of posthumous confidentiality could preclude any explanation of the "friendship" that had occurred after termination, and thus misinterpretations could prevail.

29

Many of a clinical case manager's clients with serious and persistent mental illness are members of a local advocacy group for individuals with mental illness. One of these clients asked the case manager to join them in a letter-writing effort and demonstration to oppose recently proposed budget cuts for mental health services.

1.06c; 2.05a; 6.02; 6.04

Commentary

The dilemma posed in this situation is the social worker's mandate to advocate for resources for clients as opposed to the problem of entering into a dual relationship with clients, which generally should be avoided. Even dual relationships that seem to be in the client's best interests can become complicated and negatively affect the professional relationship. Social workers do have an ethical mandate to facilitate informed participation by the public in shaping public policies. Appropriate encouragement of clients who wish to engage in letter-writing and demonstration efforts around social policy issues fits into this mandate. This can, of course, be done in other ways besides joining clients as a comrade, such as researching information, helping with strategy, and otherwise facilitating the clients' endeavor, thus fulfilling the social workers' responsibility to engage in social and political action on behalf of social justice issues.

30

A social worker in a small, predominantly Hispanic southwestern community provides case management services for older people. The community has very limited funds for these services, and individuals needing support are often referred to area cities where supported apartments and nursing homes are available. However, most of the social worker's clients want to remain in the communities in which they grew up and where their language and culture are respected and friends and family reside. The social worker knows that to help her clients remain in the community, a system of informal supports will need to be created. She hopes to talk with church leaders, shopkeepers, and other community members about helping out. She knows that to commit to help, community members will need to know something about the individuals' needs and strengths. However, she knows that the community is small and familiar and that such information could easily be linked to individuals, thus breaching her agreement of confidentiality with her clients.

1.07a; 1.03a,b; 1.05b; 6.04b,c

Commentary

The social worker must weave together a broad range of information, skills, and strategies. No ideal circumstances may be able to be effected, but she could work on several fronts. She can arrange activities and orientations to help prepare her clients for changes in housing and environments to which they will have to acclimate. Also, she could initiate measures to prepare and orient the facilities where they would be placed to some of their new clients' cultural requirements. Existing services and facilities may need to expand or modify services in accordance with the needs of a new client group. Confidentiality can become a focus of her teachings and orientations so that when she begins to make referrals, the service providers and program leaders will be prepared to honor client privacy. Perhaps members of her clientele can themselves help her plan the orientations or could aid in providing them, thus building links from an existing cohesive community to the development of new ones.

31

A first-year MSW student has a field placement at a city psychiatric hospital. Her first unsupervised intake interview is with the wife of a well-known physician, who has published many articles. During the intake, the student learns that the client has been treated over many years at various mental health facilities. Believing that all other possible forms of treatment have been exhausted without lasting success, the client's husband has recommended hospitalization, and the client has agreed. During the intake interview, the client reveals that her husband has been involved in romantic affairs with other women. The social work student completes the interview, makes a provisional diagnosis, and decides against recording specific assertions made by the woman.

1.07a; 2.05a,c; 3.04a,c

Commentary

This is the MSW student's first unsupervised intake interview, which may mean it is the first interview the student has conducted alone. She has access to a field instructor, however, and the case should be discussed carefully with the instructor. Is there anything to argue that because the client's information has not been verified and the information conveyed relates to a prominent person that extra care should be taken to protect the physician's privacy? The competence of the student to make a decision regarding what should be included in the record and to make a provisional diagnosis is questionable. The field instructor and the agency-based supervisor of the student bear ultimate responsibility for case decisions and should be involved in determining the significance of information.

The *Code of Ethics* states that social workers should not solicit private information from clients unless it is essential to the provision of service. Furthermore, information included in the record should be directly relevant to the care and treatment of the client. At the same time, social workers should keep accurate records and include sufficient information to facilitate delivery of services and ensure continuity of services. Is the wife's perception of her husband's behavior based on fact? Is her perception significant to her condition? The student should discuss the case carefully with the field instructor and consult with the agency supervisor to determine the recording procedure that is required and the usual information that is recorded. Every effort should be made to protect the rights of the client, the privacy of her husband, and the policies of the hospital.

32

A clinical social worker meets weekly for therapy with a 15-year-old female client. During a session, the client reports that she is dealing drugs and has begun seeing a boyfriend who just completed a six-month jail sentence for selling drugs. The client's parents have forbidden contact between their daughter and her boyfriend and have asked the social worker to inform them if their daughter reported that she is seeing the boy again. The social worker believes that her client trusted her not to pass on this information to anyone else and that disclosure might permanently impair the trust in their relationship. However, the social worker told her client when they first began their sessions that she could not promise to keep confidential any statements that indicate a threat to harm self or others. The social worker is concerned for her client's safety with the boyfriend but also is far more concerned about her illegal involvement in the sale of drugs and the dangers she may face from the drug trade.

1.07a,c,d; 1.01; 1.02; 1.03a

Commentary

The social worker must struggle among obligations to her primary client, a minor; to her parents, who are inevitably part of the client system; and to society, whose laws are intended to protect. She can seek to work with the client toward the goal of achieving consent to bring the parents into active work as a family unit. The social worker would endeavor to support the client and work toward accomplishing consent to reveal the relationship but with the goal of establishing a growing alliance with her parents. Or she can weigh the dangers to the client of the renewed relationship with her boyfriend plus the betrayal of the collateral clients' (the parents) expectations for the protection of their daughter and decide that revealing the information to them constitutes a compelling exception to confidentiality. If she decides on the latter course of action, the primary client (the daughter) must be informed in advance of the disclosure.

33

A client who receives services at a mental health agency notices his cousin's name on a sign-in list at the receptionist's desk. He discusses this with his social worker, saying he is uncomfortable that his cousin might also become aware that he receives treatment at the center.

1.07a,c,d,e

Commentary

Office practices are often developed by non–social workers who do not have an awareness of the rights and protections that must be accorded clients. Client confidentiality must be honored in all of the office protocols and record-keeping routines. Moreover, clients must be informed of the exceptions to confidentiality and, to the extent possible, about the necessary and inadvertent disclosures of confidential information and the expected consequences. In this instance, the client's cooperation in protecting the cousin's confidentiality should be sought as a correlate of what he can expect as protection of his own privacy. Informing the cousin of the inadvertent breach, however, would compound the problem by revealing that her relative is seeking therapy in the same setting. Can the clients be protected at least by some assurance that the professional colleagues who are delivering the services refrain from collaboration or case conferencing regarding the family, its history, and dynamics? Ideally, an agency should have a comprehensive policy in place and a systematic means of informing clients of all aspects of the policy that have implications for them.

34

A social worker in a private case management agency received a request from a national news program to document the life of a family receiving services. The social worker's supervisor is encouraging the social worker to pursue the opportunity, seeing it as a chance to shed positive light on the profession and as a marketing opportunity. The news program staff have asked that they meet and interview a consenting family just starting services and that they have access to them over a period of months for videotaped interviews to be edited and later presented on national television.

1.07a,i,k; 1.03a,f; 1.06b; 3.09c,d

Commentary

The ethics dilemma this social worker faces is a desire to enhance the public understanding of the social work profession and the reputation of the agency in conflict with breaching the privacy of the client and the confidentiality of the professional relationship. The importance of respecting clients' right to privacy and the need to protect the confidentiality of clients when responding to the requests of the media must be considered. The issue of whether consent could be truly informed should be examined, because even if the clients gave consent for the videotaping, they could not really know the impact of this videotaping of their interviews on their families. The *Code of Ethics* makes clear that because of the vulnerability of clients, social workers should not engage in solicitation of testimonial endorsements. The potential conflict with the social worker's supervisor, who is in favor of pursuing this opportunity, is dealt with in the *Code of Ethics*, which addresses the importance of not allowing the interests of the employing organization to interfere with the ethical practice of social work.

35

A residential treatment center for severely emotionally disturbed clients has developed a unique method of involving child clients in physically challenging, adventurous events to heighten self-esteem and expand the children's repertoire of physical skills and problem solving. A newspaper reporter has asked to do a series about it, with the likely results that monetary donations will escalate; others will want to replicate the program elsewhere, thus helping more children; and the journalist's reputation will be further enhanced. The center obtains general, cursory written permissions from the children's parents and guardians for the children to be observed in a range of circumstances at the facility. Once a first installment of the series is printed, two social workers observe that the children's families are depicted in malfunctional interactions with the children, and the children, who are too young to understand the implications of being identifiable, are described with intimate details of their lives and troubles. The series is nearly complete, the center's administration believes it is a worthy project, and most staff are excited about the likely publicity, but staff social workers have concerns that it may be exploitive of troubled people.

1.07b,c,d,k; 1.03a,c,f; 1.06b

Commentary

The *Code of Ethics* standards that address informed consent relate to service delivery, which is not the situation in the example. Because the series is an extension of the experience of the children in the residential center and because their "clienthood" is the focus of the articles, one must extend the logic of all of the standards that pertain to informed consent. Informed consent ideally encompasses several elements: the true nature and extent of the client's exposure, the purpose of the disclosure, the duration of the consent, and whether the client will have an opportunity to view the product and decline permission for use of portions of it. The same elements of consent should have been included in permissions by all staff and parents who would be featured as well. Having failed to obtain an acceptable level of consent and if intimate or revealing details are depicted, the journalists may be constrained from releasing the series. No doubt lawyers for the various entities will become involved in negotiating some compromise. Nonetheless, it is incumbent on the social workers to take measures to protect their clients. This could entail assessing a client's participation and what it is likely to mean in short-range treatment as well as the longer-term implications—to the extent these factors can be predicted. The articles will perhaps interpret successful treatment techniques or opportunities for severely troubled clients that are replicable and could be thought of as akin to research. The interpretive purposes of the series, where it will be published, and whether it can be legitimately argued that it will advance the public good is another dimension of analysis.

36

A psychiatrist is being sued by the parents of a married adult patient who has committed suicide. The client was also previously served by a clinical social worker. The psychiatrist's lawyers have subpoenaed the social worker's records, but he is concerned about his client's rights to privacy, because he never obtained client consent to communicate with the psychiatrist or the parents.

1.07b,c,j,r

Commentary

It is not unusual for social workers to be subpoenaed during legal proceedings involving allegations of professional malpractice. In this case, the psychiatrist's lawyers may want to see whether the social worker's records contain information that may help them defend the psychiatrist. When social workers are subpoenaed to testify or produce relevant documents or case records, social workers should not disclose confidential or privileged information without valid consent from a client or a person legally authorized to consent on behalf of a client. Social workers who seek a client's consent should be certain to explain the request in clear and understandable language and inform clients of any risks related to the disclosure, the client's right to refuse or withdraw consent, and the time frame covered by the consent.

In the case of a deceased client, what constitutes compelling professional reasons for exceptions to confidentiality may differ from considerations regarding an active client. If the psychiatrist's work or reputation are being challenged, regardless of how much information the social worker has about the psychiatrist's treatment of the client, the social worker may determine an obligation to clarify all circumstances about which she has information to both fairly advance her former client's interests and to protect a colleague from unfair consequences of his work. However, the social worker should disclose confidential information only with valid consent or as a result of a court order that she chooses not to challenge.

37

A nursing home in a small, rural town does not have Spanish-speaking professional staff but has a number of clients who speak only Spanish. The nursing home's budget is very limited, the administrator does not anticipate finding funds to hire bilingual staff, and he does not expect any staff vacancies in the near future. The nursing home employs a kitchen worker who is fluent in English and Spanish and who is willing to serve when needed as a translator during counseling sessions.

1.07c; 1.03a,b; 1.05; 1.07d; 3.07a; 3.09b,c,d; 4.02

Commentary

Available resources should always be considered by social workers and, indeed, social workers have a tradition of identifying and organizing help for clients. The requirements of confidentiality for clients should not be compromised because of a client's status or special needs, however, and it is difficult to project that the professional requirements of confidentiality and the nuances of a counseling session could be understood and honored by someone whose primary occupation is staffing a kitchen facility. Clients' comprehension must be ensured and, similarly, so should the social workers' comprehension of the clients' communication. The social workers' effectiveness would be enhanced if they were bilingual. The nursing home administrator could improve the effectiveness of services by developing incentives for the professional staff who work toward fluency in Spanish or the recruitment and training of appropriately qualified volunteers to serve as translators.

38

A clinical social worker who has lived and worked for years in a small rural town has been invited and would like to serve on boards of directors and local community action groups. Some of these groups include members whom she has served in her clinical role in the past.

1.07c; 1.06c; 5.01c

Commentary

Cross-referencing relationships are often inevitable in small towns and rural settings. Certainly, the skill and experience of a social worker would represent an important contribution and influence to local community groups. If the social worker can define her role in those circumstances quite rigidly and avoid unnecessary personal or social contact with former clients, she may indeed develop appropriate boundaries. What she inadvertently learns of former clients should be treated with discretion and disinterest. It should be presumed that when she terminated with the clients, other sources of services for the future were made known to them and they would not be reliant on returning to her for service. If, conversely, her clinical practice is still active and some of her former clients may need to return for ongoing help, she might defer her community involvement in the interest of being available if needed.

39

A clinical social worker employed in a nonprofit agency serving child victims of sexual abuse learned during a session with a seven-year-old client the identity of the man who sexually abused the client. He had not been prosecuted. Two years later the social worker sees the alleged abuser working as a janitor in a local grade school. She wants to warn the principal but knows that such a warning would require conveying information gained through a confidential session with her client. However, she feels torn because the alleged abuser is employed in a setting where he has regular access to potential victims.

1.07c; 2.05a; 6.01

Commentary

The circumstances that precluded prosecution of an alleged perpetrator of sexual abuse against a child should be investigated. Can the social worker communicate with the child protective services agency, perhaps initially without revealing the man's identity? Can the social worker corroborate the information obtained from the child—perhaps in collateral contacts with her family? Only if there is substantial evidence both that the janitor is the perpetrator and that no rehabilitative course of action was undertaken should the social worker define the circumstances as potentially dangerous. Certainly the welfare of the children in the school is a compelling issue. But the social worker should carefully consider what precautionary recommendations to make to school authorities—and whether these can be framed as a general operational policy that is not directed to one individual whose culpability may not be irrefutably established—and how they can most judiciously be conveyed.

40

A social worker employed at a juvenile correctional center has strong reason to suspect that two of the clients in the center have become sexually involved. She is aware that one of these youths is HIV positive. She knows that if she advises the non–HIV-positive youth of her partner's HIV status, the girl may likely tell others in the center. The boy is noncommittal on whether they are sexually active and, if so, whether they use appropriate protection. The social worker seeks supervision regarding the conflict between a duty to protect the girl and the client's right to confidentiality.

1.07c,d,e; 2.05a

Commentary

The social worker may not have sufficient information to justify a breach of client confidentiality on the basis of a "duty to protect," which entails intentional, foreseeable, and imminent harm. The possibility of the revelation of the boy's HIV-positive condition to the girlfriend requires some skilled clinical work with the girl both to prepare her for the possibility of receiving the information and to instill an understanding of the boundaries of confidentiality. A plan for her physical well-being and whatever decision making she may face should be established. In an institutional setting, the social worker should coordinate her planning with other professional staff. The boy must be made aware of the requirement to compromise confidentiality when another's welfare is at stake. But foremost, the social worker needs to establish the facts to the extent possible of the relationship and the risks involved.

41

A substance abuse treatment counselor who works with a client who has lost her license to drive after a recent arrest for driving while intoxicated sees the client drive to the agency for her session. During the counseling session, the social worker comes to believe that the client is under the influence of alcohol. The client shares with her social worker her frustration over her need to drive to work and other essential places as justification for her decision to occasionally drive without her license.

1.07c,d,e; 2.05a

Commentary

The standard exceptions to confidentiality include disclosure of information shared by a client when it is necessary to prevent serious, foreseeable, and imminent harm to a client or other identifiable person or when laws, such as mandatory laws to report child abuse, require disclosure without a client's consent. A social worker should be knowledgeable about or obtain proper consultation about relevant laws and regulations concerning disclosure. One might argue that the loss of one's driver's permit—unlikely as a consequence of a first offense—constitutes a dangerous situation and holds the possibility of harm to the client or an innocent other. In a setting that regularly treats substance abusers, however, the agency should have definitive policies in place regarding confidentiality and the circumstances that can lead to disclosure of information without consent. So one should be able to presume that the client is aware that her disclosure could be reported or acted on. The social worker will have to do an objective assessment of the client's state of functioning and her reliability in making and following through on a plan to rectify her wrongdoing and get her life and treatment back on track. In the absence of a strong assurance of that outcome, the social worker may have to notify a law enforcement agency immediately or take other measures to prevent the client from continuing to drive while intoxicated and without a permit. This, however, should come as no surprise to the client. The client's problem of needing transportation to work should be addressed as a separate but important issue.

42

A private clinical practitioner in a small town keeps her client notes and billing information on the computer that is locked in her office. On returning to her office after a long weekend, she discovers that the computer has been stolen. She believes she has good reason to suspect a specific client of the theft. She needs to report the theft to the police to make an insurance claim to help replace the equipment. Reporting the suspect may require disclosure to the police of his status as her client. She also wonders if she should inform other clients of the theft, knowing that the possible revelation of confidential information may cause some of them grave concern.

1.07c,d,e,l; 3.04c

Commentary

The social worker has an obligation to notify each client whose records are on her computer of the theft because she can no longer assure them of confidentiality because of circumstances beyond her control. She also needs to evaluate if she has taken reasonable steps to ensure that her records were stored in a secure location and if her documentation included only information relevant to the delivery of service. Perhaps the social worker should initially assess the quality of her "evidence" or suspicions that a particular client was responsible for the theft; has the client a history of antisocial behavior? Were there issues that the client was dealing with that would suggest he or she needed money or would act out against the social worker? She should weigh her reasons to determine whether there is a compelling rationale for providing investigators with identifying information about the suspected client. Finally, she should weigh the responsibility to inform the suspected client of the anticipated disclosure with the possible consequences of doing so.

43

Social workers regularly discuss client progress and receive supervision at a community mental health center's weekly case review. In the case review, a social worker reports that her client has recently discovered that he is HIV positive, and she requests help in considering changes in his treatment plan in light of this information. Another social worker, who is treating the wife of the recently diagnosed HIV-positive client, learns of her client's husband's HIV status because she attends the same case review. She knows that the couple is having unprotected sex and that the wife is unaware of her husband's HIV status.

1.07c,d,q; 2.05a

Commentary

The value of confidentiality is frequently challenged in providing services to clients. Although social workers should protect the confidentiality of a client, there are limitations, and the possibility of an exception should be addressed with the male client. The social workers participating in the case review are obligated to keep confidential all cases discussed, yet there may exist sufficient compelling reason to breach a client's confidence. The exception that requires a disclosure to prevent serious, foreseeable, and imminent harm to the client's wife must be considered as a basis of the social worker's decision making. The client's wife is at high risk of becoming HIV positive, thus providing a compelling reason to breach confidentiality. In working with the husband, the social worker needs to provide information, incentive, and details about her obligation to breach his confidentiality if the client takes no steps to inform and protect his wife.

44

A social worker's client began stalking the social worker after their professional relationship terminated. The social worker took precautions such as moving to a new apartment and changing her personal telephone number, but the client has located her and continues to leave mildly threatening telephone messages and to send messages almost daily by certified and regular mail. The social worker is now considering seeking a restraining order against her client. However, she will need to disclose his status as a former client to obtain the restraining order and might be asked to provide further details about his personal history.

1.07c,e; 2.05a

Commentary

The social worker should review case record notes and perhaps confer with any other professionals for whom she had consent to collaborate by the client. She could explore whether there are any other likely means to end the client's behavior directed toward her and whether her conclusion that it is a particular client who is engaging in the behavior is verifiable. She certainly has the right to take measures to protect herself but should reveal the least amount of information about the client necessary to accomplish that goal.

45

A school social worker receives a memorandum from the school superintendent describing a new policy for reports of suspected child abuse. In the memo, the superintendent explains that he must be informed of suspected abuse and review the student's case file before a report is made to the child protective services agency. The memo explains that the reason for this new policy is to allow the superintendent time to review the social worker's record of the student before the abuse is reported.

1.07c,e,q; 3.09c,d

Commentary

A client's confidentiality has limitations. For compelling reasons, such as the suspected abuse of a child, confidentiality may be broken if the limitations or reasons are explained to the client. However, the superintendent's recently instituted policy to review the social work record before the reporting of the suspected abuse in conjunction with mandated reporting laws is not a compelling reason to breach a client's confidences. Another ethics standard to keep in mind is that social workers should not disclose identifying information when discussing case material with consultants—one way of describing the superintendent—without consent of the client. The social worker confronted with a new policy that would place her in opposition to her professional code of ethics has a responsibility to work to modify the policy.

46

A social worker who specializes in marriage and family counseling sometimes works with couples who decide to divorce. In one such case, the social worker receives a subpoena to provide testimony regarding his sessions with the divorcing couple. The husband's lawyer has recommended that the social worker be asked to give a deposition, and the wife and her attorney have agreed; both have provided signed consents for release of information. In his sessions with the husband, the social worker learned that the husband had had an affair that his attorney is unaware of. Although the social worker does not believe it is in the husband's interest that he testify, he considers that he is being ordered "by a court of law or other legally authorized body" to disclose "confidential or privileged information."

1.07d,e,f,g,j; 1.06d

Commentary

It is not unusual for social workers to be subpoenaed to testify about their contact with clients. As in this case, social workers may be subpoenaed in conjunction with divorce proceedings. As a general rule, social workers should not disclose confidential information without their clients' consent or unless they have been ordered to do so by a court of law. If a court of law or other legally authorized body orders social workers to disclose confidential or privileged information without a client's consent and such disclosure could cause harm to the client, social workers should request that the court withdraw or limit the order.

In this particular case, the social worker should have discussed with the husband the possibility that the social worker's knowledge of the husband's affair, if disclosed during the deposition, could be harmful to the husband's legal interests. The social worker should have given the husband an opportunity to consider this possible consequence when the social worker obtained the husband's informed consent for the social worker to testify. The requirement to inform clients of the limitations of confidentiality applies whether social workers disclose confidential information on the basis of a legal requirement or with client consent. In addition, social workers who provide services to two or more people who have a relationship with each other, such as couples, should clarify with all parties which individuals will be considered clients and the possibility of conflicts of interest among them.

47

A social worker is employed by a managed care firm that requires total access to client records. The social worker contends that it is not necessary to provide comprehensive information regarding his clients to the third-party payers. However, his supervisor has advised him that, without information deemed "sufficient" by the managed care company, he may not be authorized to provide treatment over the number of sessions he recommends as necessary for his clients.

1.07d,e,h; 3.09a,c,d; 6.04a

Commentary

Under these circumstances, clients must be informed at the time of initial contact of the company's requirement of "total access" to their records. Then the clients can either give written consent or seek services elsewhere before revealing significant information. However, another issue for the social worker is that by accepting employment in an organization in which the practices violate his perception of clients' rights to privacy and confidentiality, he has placed himself in an ethically conflictual situation. Social workers are expected to adhere to commitments made to employers, including abiding by their policies, but should not allow the organization to interfere with their ethical practice of social work. The social worker should consider strategies available to negotiate a different agreement between his employing agency and the managed care company or to work collectively with advocates for modifications in managed care requirements.

48

A female private practitioner has become aware of a male client's sexual attraction to her. She believes he often misinterprets her words or gestures in sexual terms and fears he may make sexual overtures toward her. She is also concerned that he might misinterpret her words or actions and lodge a complaint against her for sexual impropriety. She is considering referring him to another therapist but prefers not to do this because there has been good therapeutic progress. The social worker is struggling to maintain clear boundaries and to protect herself and her client.

1.09a; 1.06c; 2.05a,c; 2.06a

Commentary

In this situation, the practitioner should seek immediate consultation to determine if her decision to continue service to this client is in his best interests. If through consultation it is determined that continuing therapy with him is imperative, then the consultant can support her in maintaining clear boundaries to protect herself and the client. During the consultation, the practitioner should disclose only the information necessary for the consultant to understand the issue and make the client aware of her consultative arrangements. The practitioner seems to be very aware of the risks of a dual relationship, including the idea that the client might misinterpret her words or actions as being of a sexual nature. Consultation can assist her in clarifying her role and the dynamics of the professional relationship.

49

A social worker in a long-term-care facility for elderly people frequently does collateral work with family members of residents. Last year she worked with the adult children of a terminally ill patient about financial arrangements. She referred the son to a private social work practitioner to work on his issues of grief and loss and unresolved anger toward siblings. The social worker from the residential care facility and the son later encountered each other at a museum-sponsored class. They had coffee following the last class session and talked about happenings since the elderly client died. Soon thereafter, they pursued other social contact, which eventually evolved into a romance and sexual intimacy.

1.09a,b,c; 1.01; 1.06a,b,c,d

Commentary

This case provides an example of a potentially serious conflict of interest. Although the social worker has not become socially and sexually involved with a primary client, having referred the primary client's son to another practitioner, there is clear potential for a conflict of interest, because the son had been part of the client system. The man is a former client in one respect, in that he has been referred to another provider. As a matter of principle, the social worker has an obligation not to enter into a sexual relationship with a current or former client, or a client's relative, because of the potential harm to the client. The social worker's intimate relationship with the patient's son could interfere with the exercise of professional discretion and impartial judgment if there were to be ongoing service needs. Should the social worker and the son remain involved, the social worker could, in principle, benefit directly from decisions that a patient and family made with respect to the financial issues the social worker discussed with family members. This is a potential conflict of interest. In addition, it is not hard to imagine that other family members, part of the family constellation, might feel deeply betrayed by the intimate relationship between the social worker and the client's son.

50

A social worker who administers a school social work program occasionally has group sessions with parents of children who are being seen on an ongoing basis by her staff social workers. The administrator generally makes herself available for interpretation and information and referral work for the parents. Following several professional contacts with the divorced father of one of the children that are followed by an informal extension of the discussion over coffee, she and he embark on a personal relationship and eventually marry.

1.09c; 1.06a,b,c; 2.05a,c

Commentary

Social workers who administer social services programs and supervise social workers have the same ethical obligations as do the direct practice social workers. The development of a dual relationship between an administrator and a client jeopardizes the social worker's ability to maintain sound judgment about the father of a child being served by one of her supervisees. At the outset of the personal relationship, the administrator had an obligation to inform her supervisees of the circumstances and take appropriate measures to minimize any effects. The consultation of those colleagues should have guided her in her actions and decision making. She must be assured that no detrimental effects for the child client could ensue.

51

While they were undergraduate students together, two male students were sexually involved for about one year. Seven years have passed since the two have seen each other when one of the men learns that the other man has earned an MSW and is practicing at the local mental health center. He asks his former lover to take him as a client, explaining that he is ending a relationship and wants to examine his relationship patterns. He feels that the social worker is uniquely qualified to be especially helpful because of his intimate knowledge of him, coupled with his clinical training.

1.09d; 1.06c

Commentary

Although the clinical social worker has the experience and professional education necessary to provide the service, it is not in anyone's best interest to do so unless a dual relationship is completely unavoidable—that is, no other qualified mental health practitioner is available within a reasonable distance. The guiding standard must be that a social worker does not provide services to an individual with whom he has had a prior sexual relationship. This past history makes it difficult to maintain appropriate professional boundaries and to objectively focus on the client's true issues. The prospective mental health provider can present a range of appropriate referral information.

52

An interior decorator has asked a private social work practitioner to contract with her for therapy in exchange for interior design services. The social worker, who is just establishing herself in private practice, has meager earnings to date and prefers a barter economy. She has been successful in using her skills in trade for most things she needs. The client has traded and had commissions for her work and can approximate the value of her work. She is willing to contract for specific services or hours of service in keeping with the social worker's preferences that are comparable in value to the number of sessions they undertake. The social worker has been planning to redo her home, has seen the client's portfolio, and likes her work.

1.13a,b; 1.06b,c

Commentary

As a general rule, social workers should avoid accepting goods or services from clients as payment for professional services. Although bartering may be permissible in extraordinary circumstances, it should be avoided because it creates the potential for conflicts of interest, exploitation, and inappropriate boundaries in social workers' relationships with their clients. Consider, for example, how the quality of the social worker–client relationship could be compromised and damaged if the social worker is not satisfied with some aspect of the client's decorating services. A dispute between the parties concerning some defect in materials or labor could certainly undermine the client's therapy. In addition, the social worker's dependence on the client's expertise and availability as a result of this dual relationship could introduce complex clinical dynamics that could be detrimental to the client's therapy. It is always questionable whether a "perfect" exchange in services can be achieved; it is inherently unlikely that there will be equal quantities of need and service.

Social workers should explore and may participate in bartering only in very limited circumstances when it can be demonstrated that such arrangements are an accepted practice among professionals in the local community and considered to be essential for the provision of services. Wherever possible, social workers should explore alternative fee arrangements or referral to another provider when a bartering arrangement creates the potential for a conflict of interest and inappropriate boundaries.

53

A school social worker provides clinical services to a number of children with disabilities in the school setting. In light of budget constraints and aware that some services performed by school social workers could be billed to Medicaid, the principal has asked the social worker to bill Medicaid for her work with students with disabilities. The social worker feels caught among wanting to serve students; helping the school stretch its tight budget; and her concern that she is being asked to "double bill," because funds authorized by federal legislation pay for social work done with students with disabilities.

1.13c; 3.09d; 4.04

Commentary

The *Code of Ethics* can be helpful to the social worker in dealing with the competing demands in her agency. The first ethical standard to consider is that social workers should not solicit remuneration for providing services to clients who are entitled to the same services through the social worker's agency. Further, if the social worker educates the principal about the ethical standards of the profession, she can join with the principal by ensuring that she is a diligent steward of the resources of the agency.

54

A social worker employed in a well-respected sectarian mental health agency met with his supervisor to discuss treatment of an HIV-positive adolescent client's disclosure that he has anonymous sex with men. The following week the social worker's supervisor, espousing agency policy—whether formal or informal—advised him that his client's case must be closed because he poses a safety risk to the other adolescents in the program and because the agency's reputation could be tarnished for serving gay boys with AIDS.

1.16b; 3.07d; 3.09c,d; 4.02; 6.04b

Commentary

The central conflict is the client's right to treatment regardless of sexual orientation and the social worker's obligation to the agency. A sectarian agency has a legal right to develop policies according to its religious beliefs. However, the social worker has a professional obligation not to discriminate against a client based on sexual orientation. In terms of the mission of a mental health agency that employs social workers and other mental health professionals, how the agency could morally justify discrimination by refusing services to this client should be questioned. The manner in which it is doing so amounts to a requirement that the social worker abandon the client. This has both ethical and legal implications. The sectarian organization, by the nature of its mission grounded both in social work values and religious values, should be helped to recognize its moral responsibility to this client. The *Code of Ethics* requires that social workers, as a part of their commitment to employers, inform them of their ethical obligation as prescribed by the *Code*. Moreover, the social worker has the responsibility to help administrators create a work environment that helps their employees carry out their ethical responsibilities.

In situations such as these, the social worker may have to consider whether he or she can continue employment with an agency where there is a conflict between one's professional values and an agency's prerogatives. Religious agencies should make their policies based on religious values and how these are expected to be carried out in practice clear at the time of contracting with an employee. All of the relevant facts are needed to determine one's ethical action; the situation suggests the need for consultation.

55

During the 10th of 12 sessions, a private clinical social worker and his group began planning for termination in keeping with the managed care provider's authorization to cover only 12 sessions. The social worker met with one group member individually to discuss the client's uncertainty that his therapeutic work would actually be completed by that time. The group member could not afford individual therapy, and his insurance would not cover it. The clinician has considered providing pro bono services but must weigh this against the possibility that such an agreement might set up an expectation by the other clients, some of whom might choose to continue on an individual basis as well.

1.16b,e; 6.04a

Commentary

Because the therapeutic arrangement was for 12 sessions, there is not a precipitous ending. However, the social worker does have the responsibility for helping all group members determine their readiness for ending. For a client who is not prepared to terminate, the clinician needs to provide information regarding transfer to another clinician; referral to an agency with a sliding-scale fee system; or the justification, including financial, for continuing with the client. In addition, the clinical social worker, through his professional organizations, should work toward influencing the managed care provider to expand coverage.

56

A social worker in a sectarian family agency, who had long-standing differences with the agency regarding policy issues, resigned his position, giving two months' notice. The agency immediately informed him that his employment was terminated and that he would be precluded from any further contact with clients. The social worker feels he is being prevented from terminating appropriately with his clients but knows that he would need to take telephone numbers or addresses from client files with him if he were to decide unilaterally to engage in termination contacts.

1.16b,e,f; 1.07n; 3.09a,b,c,d

Commentary

This issue reflects a conflict between the right of the client to adequate service and the duty of the social worker to provide this as opposed to the agency's right or authority to terminate the worker. In attempting to contact the clients, the worker risks legal action, which has been taken in a few cases. One would question whether the worker has tried to resolve this issue, as well as the termination of his position, within the agency. His responsibility to his clients needs to be framed as an ethics issue. The social worker needs to inform the agency administration of his ethical obligation in this regard and to make him or her aware of the *Code of Ethics*, which is a part of his commitment to his employer. The social worker should not "abandon" clients who are still in need of the services. Because the agency setting is a sectarian organization, the worker could appeal to the agency on moral grounds.

The social worker has the additional obligation to help the organization carry out its services ethically and work toward improving its policies and procedures. It should be pointed out that the organization has not only an ethical responsibility to clients in terms of its workers' terminating clients but also a legal responsibility. It is therefore within the best interests of both the agency and the clients to have this worker terminate service with his clients in an appropriate manner. The social worker should advocate within and outside the agency to meet clients' needs. This assumes that the social worker uses change strategies, such as collaboration and negotiation, skillfully. Good practice skills often preclude ethics conflicts, or at least help resolve them amicably. Regarding the issue of the social worker's employment being terminated, the social worker could appeal the termination of employment within the organization if there is a grievance procedure in place.

57

A managed care mental health center recently placed new, more restrictive limits on the number of sessions clients can receive in a calendar year. A social worker employee of the center, who also has a private psychotherapy practice, believes that the time period is too short for at least three of her clients and reports that each would like to continue seeing her. She would like to let them know that she has a private practice and would be willing to continue providing services to them in that setting as paying clients.

1.16e; 1.06b; 1.15

Commentary

The social worker who anticipates the termination of services to clients should notify clients and provide for the continuation of services in relation to the client's needs and preferences by transfer or referral. At the same time, the social worker must be mindful not to further her business interests. The social worker should fully discuss all options available and appropriate to each client for continuation of services, taking care to avoid any conflict of interest.

2. Social Workers' Ethical Responsibilities to Colleagues

58

The social worker manager of the pretrial unit of a forensic department at a large state psychiatric hospital oversees the work of seven social workers and a dozen psychiatric aides. A licensed social worker, he was hired five years ago, does exemplary work, and receives excellent performance evaluations. A social worker on the unit was recently widowed, and her friendship with the pretrial unit manager—her supervisor—has evolved into a romance. The hospital administrator believes it is risky for a manager to have a personal relationship with a supervisee. The unit manager argues that they have maintained the same level of professionalism that has existed for the years they have worked together and that their personal and professional lives are kept completely separate. The administrator, a psychiatrist, has set up separate meetings with the social worker and the manager and intends to grill them on the potential implications of their romance and to propose reassigning the social worker to a chronic ward—a population with which she has had no experience or specialized training.

2.07a; 3.01c; 4.01a

Commentary

The *Code of Ethics* states unequivocally that someone who exercises authority over another should not engage in an intimate relationship with the supervisee. Regardless of what clear boundaries the social workers may believe they can establish, other perceptions of favoritism, special treatment, and less-than-objective decision making will undermine an effective work unit. Moreover, the dual relationship could ultimately lead to harm to the supervisee's career if the personal relationship goes sour. A reassignment of the supervisee already would appear to be unfair treatment, if she does not have a sufficient level of competence or a desire to work in another unit. Whether the supervisee can retain the position she desires and be supervised by someone other than the manager should be explored. Few would argue that the personal relationship which, as described, does not seem to be inherently exploitive, should be abandoned.

59

Two social workers have been friends for nearly 20 years. One is a solo clinical practitioner and has never sought to become licensed or to join any professional organizations. The solo practitioner confides in her social worker friend that she is actively sexually involved with a client whom she has diagnosed as clinically depressed and for whom she receives insurance reimbursement for fees.

2.11a,b,c,d; 1.06c; 1.09a; 5.01a

Commentary

Because there are *no circumstances* that justify sexual activity between the social worker and her client, the social worker friend must advise the solo practitioner that she is engaging in unprofessional and unethical (and in some cases illegal) conduct. Even though this confrontation may jeopardize their friendship, the social worker receiving this information must strive to promote high standards of practice.

In this case, because the solo practitioner is neither licensed nor a member of a professional organization, the social worker needs to obtain information from the local authorities—that is, the district attorney's office—regarding possible civil or criminal actions. Once in possession of the information, the social worker should advise the practitioner of the potential risks to herself and her professional future if she does not correct this situation. There is the potential for involving the insurance company, because the solo practitioner would have signed a contract with it that states specific policies and practices.

60

When allegations of sexual abuse were made against a social worker, the county's child protective services (CPS) agency investigated and concluded that the charges were unfounded. The social worker advised her employing agency of the county's investigation and of the fact that she was exonerated. CPS also sent a letter to the agency confirming the investigation and the social worker's exoneration. However, the investigation yielded information from earlier periods regarding the social worker's confidentiality breaches and her sexual involvement with an adult client. The social worker who investigated the allegations is unsure whether she has responsibility or authority to initiate action against the social worker or to advise the social worker's agency about the other infractions.

2.11a,b,c,d; 1.07c

Commentary

The investigating social worker believes that she has a source of authoritative information that may affect the fitness for service of a social worker in another agency. Yet the investigator is bound to take action only with regard to the question before the CPS agency. The record available to her may not contain information regarding whether appropriate corrective actions had been undertaken in conjunction with the earlier offenses. She may have no means of legitimately obtaining that information. Furthermore, there may be no established procedure for handling concerns about the colleague's conduct in these circumstances. Neither of the exceptions to confidentiality—the duty to take action to protect the client or a designated other or a mandatory reporting law—applies in these circumstances. The investigating social worker may have to suppress her urge to take some sort of action, because none that is appropriate and ethical is available.

3. Social Workers' Ethical Responsibilities in Practice Settings

61

A social worker employed in a mid-sized community's state psychiatric hospital is supervised by the grandmother of one of her outpatient clients. The other qualified supervisor is the close colleague of her supervisor. The social worker felt obliged to report to the local child protective services (CPS) agency that the young client, the supervisor's granddaughter, appeared abused. CPS investigated and made plans to move the child to her grandmother's home. The social worker feels caught among the desire not to disrupt services to the emotionally disturbed child, the worker's need for supervision in all cases, and colleagues' warnings against the potential dual relationship with her supervisor.

3.01c; 1.06a

Commentary

The central ethics concern in this case is the professional responsibility of the social worker to avoid dual roles in the supervisory relationship and her right to qualified supervision. The *Code of Ethics* proscribes such relationships when there is risk of exploitation or potential harm to the supervisee. Potentially, the worker would be involved in the personal life of the grandmother if she continues to be active in the case of this child, who now is in the grandmother's, her supervisor's, home. Alternatives to this plan should be considered carefully. The child could be transferred to another worker within the psychiatric facility, assuming that the referral arrangements are handled thoughtfully, that the worker's supervisor would not have a conflict of interest, and that the skills and competence of the colleague are appropriate to the child's needs. The social worker must assiduously guard the confidentiality of the child and what she has learned about the child's circumstances. Conversely, the qualified supervisor who is a close friend of the grandmother may be able to assume the supervisory responsibility. In such a case, the boundaries of the supervisory relationship should be made clear.

62

A social work student who is a member of a small religious community hopes to do her field placement at the agency run by the religious community. The field instructor for this placement would be the individual whom the student has relied on as a "spiritual director" for the past two years. Because of her role as the student's spiritual director, the social worker has in-depth knowledge of the personal and spiritual issues the student has faced. Both the student and her spiritual director feel comfortable with the prospect of adding a supervisory element to their relationship.

3.02a,d

Commentary

Although recognizing emerging interest in spirituality as an element of direct practice, social work educators generally would hesitate to place a student in an organization run by the religious community in which the student is a member. In this situation, the religious community is a small one, and the student no doubt has multiple relationships with various members and possibly within this agency. Assuming competence on the part of the agency and the field instructor as is required of social work educators and assuming that the circumstances suggest that this is a suitable placement for this student, there is a serious question about assigning her to a field instructor who has been her spiritual director for two years. This involves a dual role relationship. As field instructor, the social work practitioner–educator is bound by the *Code of Ethics* to model ethical behavior to students. The social work role and the role of spiritual director are distinct and have different purposes. The role of a spiritual director is to help the directee discern the action and direction of a higher power in the life of the person. Contemporary spiritual direction does draw heavily from the behavioral sciences, especially psychology. Although distinct from therapy, spiritual guidance may entail much personal knowledge of the directee that could interfere with the educational process and place the student at risk. The length of the established relationship suggests it may be difficult for the field instructor and the student to shift roles.

In making a decision to place the student in this agency, the school should carefully consider all possible consequences and all alternative options. If further information would suggest that this placement would be appropriate for this student and a more appropriate field placement was not available, it would be important that the field instructor not carry out her role as field instructor and spiritual director simultaneously. A lack of clarity as to the purpose of social work could not only be confusing to the student but also could provide the student with an inadequate educational experience. If this field placement is used for the student, it would be important that the field instructor set clear professional boundaries.

63

A professor of social work has a student in two classes and is her practicum supervisor–instructor at the mental health clinic where he works part-time. On the basis of personal statement papers, class comments, and revelations in supervisory sessions, the student has disclosed information about many personal circumstances that have interactive effects in her pursuit of the social work degree. Based on that information, the professor has offered clinical observations of her behavior and, at times, has assumed a therapeutic role with her.

3.02d; 1.03a; 3.01c

Commentary

Social work educators must avoid entering into inappropriate dual and multiple relationships with their students. This is particularly important in light of the authority that educators have over students with respect to grades, field work evaluations, and letters of recommendation to potential employers. Social work educators, for example, should not provide clinical or psychotherapeutic services to their students. This would constitute an unacceptable mixing of professional roles and could be harmful to students. It is likely that students who are also receiving psychotherapeutic services from their professors would be confused about the nature of their relationship and that this confusion would interfere with the students' learning and their clinical progress. Social work educators and field instructors are responsible for setting clear and appropriate boundaries.

The prohibition concerning dual and multiple relationships does not mean, however, that social work educators should not draw on their clinical knowledge and expertise in an effort to assist students who struggle with personal issues that affect their learning. Educators who become aware of students' personal problems may use their clinical expertise to help students identify issues that warrant attention and help students locate appropriate service providers (for example, student mental health services or information and referral services in the community). Social work educators must be careful to limit their involvement to helping students identify relevant issues and locate professional assistance; educators should not counsel students or suggest to students that they are available to provide clinical services.

64

A supervisor had been concerned about a staff social worker's job performance and attitude for some time. The supervisee was erratic in her performance, was scattered in her efforts to accomplish tasks, and appeared to be distracted by unidentifiable stimuli. Informally, there seemed to be "mental health difficulties." The social worker and her husband had been awaiting the scheduled surgery of their seven-year-old child. In an effort to contribute to the positive and supportive atmosphere for the child and to avoid making her staffer feel threatened that her performance was inadequate and her job in jeopardy, the supervisor deferred preparing the usual annual performance evaluation. Six months later, the social worker's performance has improved somewhat, but her attendance is dismal and excuses for absence transparently contrived. The supervisor believes she should document the earlier performance, which would be negative, and describe the attendance problem, too.

3.03; 2.09a,b

Commentary

The social work supervisor, by attempting to be supportive of the supervisee, is neglecting the service needs of the clients of the supervisee. By delaying her evaluation of the social worker, the supervisor prevented the social worker from taking remedial action sooner and preserving her job. Social workers who have responsibility for evaluating others should do so in a fair and timely manner. The evaluation criteria should reflect the requirements of the job. In addition, if social workers have knowledge of a social work colleague's impairment, they should consult with that colleague and help him or her take action and seek help.

65

An employee assistance program social worker was counseling a mother, primarily around family issues, while a colleague provided services to the children. Aware that the mother's allotted insurance coverage was nearly exhausted, the therapists proposed to bill the insurer under the children's names because they have more extended benefits.

3.05; 1.01; 4.04; 6.04a

Commentary

An overarching ethics standard is the social worker's commitment to clients, with the client's interest being the primary concern of the social worker. A social worker might embrace this standard to justify obtaining needed services for a client by submitting inaccurate billing information to the insurance company. However, the social worker must balance the client's interests with the requirement that billing must accurately reflect the nature and extent of services and identify who provided the service. The social workers could legitimately advocate for appropriate reimbursement for the services provided to and required by the mother.

66

Social workers in a hospital will be rewarded in their role as case managers for helping to generate revenue. It is intended that third-party reimbursement funds will become a more prevalent source of income for the hospital. The social workers may thus be forced into the position of giving preference to privately insured clients and providing less service to Medicaid and Medicare patients.

3.07b,d; 1.06a,b; 3.09b,c,d; 5.01a; 6.04b

Commentary

The *Code of Ethics* clearly states that social workers should advocate for fair and nondiscriminatory resource allocation procedures. Giving preferential treatment to clients on the basis of fiscal reimbursement is discriminatory. These social workers face an ethics dilemma by being asked to allow the employing organization's fiscal needs to interfere with their ethical practice of social work. Administrators should endeavor to eliminate any conditions in their organization that interfere with their social work staff's compliance with their professional code of ethics. By providing a financial incentive to the social workers to help the hospital generate revenue, these administrators have placed the social workers in a potential conflict of interest between fair, impartial treatment of clients and their own and agency interests. Moreover, social workers are expected to expand choice and opportunity for less-advantaged groups.

67

A mental health center referred a client with homicidal and suicidal ideation to a private practitioner with whom the agency has a contractual relationship. The practitioner receives no regular supervision or consultation and, based on experience and training, does not feel competent to work with this client. The agency reports that it cannot offer supervision or consultation regarding the case because of the excessive demand on its professional resources.

3.07c; 1.04a; 2.05a; 2.06a

Commentary

The ethics conflict for the social worker lies in the *Code's* proscription against working with clients outside one's area of specialized knowledge or expertise versus the social worker's need to make a living. The social worker can interpret to the administrator of the mental health center the ethics requirement that administrators should take reasonable steps to ensure that appropriate staff supervision is provided and that it is ethically impossible for the practitioner to accept this referral.

68

An adult client with a physical disability and mental retardation resides in a group home. His parents are his legal guardians. They remain in contact with him and visit him every three months. The client has some difficulty walking and uses a shower chair because of his disability. Recently, the client slipped in his bathtub and injured his leg and ankle. He received immediate medical treatment and is recovering well. He is embarrassed about the fall and does not want his parents to know about it. The social worker believes he should advise the client's parents of the injury. Concerned about possible lawsuits or investigations of "neglect," the agency director suggests that because the client is recovering there is no need to inform the parents. The agency policy regarding parental or guardian involvement is ambiguous about this sort of incident.

3.09d; 1.02; 1.06d; 1.07b,c

Commentary

The social worker is experiencing an ethics conflict in his relationship with his clients and with his employer. The social worker should be mindful that when providing services to two or more people who have a relationship with each other, it is important to clarify his role and his professional responsibilities to the involved parties. In addition, the social worker should not allow the employer's policy and practice to interfere with ethical social work practice. The social worker may use the opportunity to educate his employer about social work professional ethics and work to make clear the policy of the agency. The agency case record must reflect that the primary client declined to give consent for his parents to be informed. Whether a supervisor's opinion or the direct service provider's judgment prevails should be addressed as a rational administrative protocol.

4. Social Workers' Ethical Responsibilities as Professionals

69

A state foster care social worker coordinated an emergency foster placement for a teenage girl in the home of two women. The agency asked the women to continue the placement as regular foster parents. In the course of the home study, the women disclosed their lesbian orientation to the social worker and let her know that they were partners. The couple asked that the social worker not report the nature of their relationship to the court. The social worker believes that the judge will not allow placement of a child in the home of a lesbian couple but also knows that the women provide excellent care for the teenager, who has developed a good relationship with them.

4.02; 1.01; 1.07a,c; 4.04; 6.04a,b

Commentary

There is conflict in this case between the rights of the foster family to be free from discrimination and the public policy, implicit or explicit, that would deny them the right to apply as a foster family. One could argue that the court has a right to exercise such a policy, perhaps based on the standards of the community, and therefore would have a right to this information. The social worker, then, may be faced with an additional conflict—truth telling and the privacy rights of the client. One could question whether the court has a right to this information. However, this case may provide the opportunity to advocate for change. This would be in keeping with the ethics requirement that social workers not practice, condone, facilitate, or collaborate with any form of discrimination that includes sexual orientation. This approach would be within the context of the mission of social work and requirements that social workers engage in social and political action in such cases. The risk of losing an effective foster home and creating a circumstance in which the teenager might be moved to a different placement must be weighed in the examination of priorities. Clearly, this type of case may offer the possibility of engaging authorities in an ethics dialogue that could lead to change. The social worker should have knowledge of the court and the community and should receive consultation. The skilled use of strategies for change could effectively influence policy.

70

A therapist for a nonprofit mental health agency believes the agency engages in racially discriminatory practices in their service delivery—for example, determination of eligibility, assignment to staff, length of waiting time for initial visits, and so forth. The social worker's previous efforts to address these concerns with the agency administration have been fruitless. After discussing these concerns with colleagues, she considers making public excerpts of agency records without the agency's permission, but disguising all identifying information regarding clients.

4.02; 3.07b,d; 3.09a,b,c,d; 6.04a,b,c,d

Commentary

Opposing discrimination wherever it is found is a strong theme of the *Code of Ethics*, including in the practices of the social worker's employing organization. The *Code* does mandate that agency administrators not engage in racially discriminatory practices. Thus, in this situation the social worker correctly feels the urgency of taking some corrective action. However, agency records do belong to the agency, and taking them without permission does violate the sections of the *Code* that require social workers to adhere to commitments made to employers and employing organizations. The social workers should find other means to continue pursuing this equity matter, including advocating in the political arena.

71

A social worker employed at an organ transplant center for a number of years has suspected a pattern of discrimination in selection of transplant candidates. Administrative staff at the center have denied the possibility of discrimination. Over a two-year period, the social worker has collected data proving that the organization has a pattern of discrimination in its referral process. The social worker has met with the medical director, who suggested that her data are wrong and advised her that an external investigation of allegations of this nature would interfere with the efficient delivery of needed transplant services at the center.

4.02; 3.09b,c,d; 5.02a; 6.04a,b

Commentary

The social worker should organize her data into an official research report and present it to the appropriate authority. As collegial courtesy, the social worker should inform the medical director of her intentions to use the data in an effort to establish fair policies that are assiduously adhered to. The basis of the existing agency policy should be objectively evaluated and, if demonstrably unfair, the social worker should advocate for change that follows a careful, thoughtful strategy. Her own job status could be jeopardized, and the possible consequences of her actions should be understood.

72

A client has struggled for years with bipolar disorder. He is under the care of a psychiatrist and on appropriate medication but remains actively symptomatic most of the time. He lives with an elderly mother who has a meager pension. Occasionally during brief periods of stability he manages to obtain part-time work, but the work is usually short lived. A social worker is helping him apply for disability support, but the brief part-time work, if officially reported, would make him ineligible. The work has generally been informal (that is, not connected with social security or any other benefits). The social worker is contemplating whether it is fraudulent or deceitful to discourage the client from reporting the brief work stints in order for him to demonstrate eligibility for disability.

4.04; 6.01; 6.04a,b

Commentary

The situation involves a conflict between the well-being and welfare of the client and his mother and the duty of the social worker to uphold the law. It is the duty of the social worker not to participate in, condone, or be associated with dishonesty, fraud, or deception. To act otherwise could compromise not only the integrity of the individual social worker but also the profession. On the other hand, society has an obligation to meet the needs of vulnerable and disadvantaged people, and social workers have an obligation to act to expand choice and opportunity for all people but with special regard for the vulnerable, oppressed, and disadvantaged populations. In this case, the social worker has the responsibility to help the client make an informed judgment about the course of his action and carefully consider with him the possible consequences of failing to report his part-time work. At the same time, the social worker should be actively involved in advocating for the clients and in participating in efforts, through her agency and NASW, to promote social policies that appropriately respond to the needs of clients with physical or mental disabilities.

73

A licensed clinical social worker regularly receives treatment from a psychiatrist and takes medication, as prescribed, for depression. She and her psychiatrist agree that she is fully capable of serving her clients effectively. As a private clinician, she needs to apply for membership on provider panels. One application asks if she has ever had a diagnosis for a mental illness.

4.05a,b; 4.04

Commentary

It appears that this clinician's mental health problem is being treated and monitored in a very appropriate manner. Because it would be unethical and inappropriate for her to misrepresent herself to the provider panel, she could indicate her diagnosis and submit a statement from her psychiatrist describing her treatment and his assessment of her capability to serve her clients.

74

A multiservice family agency has had a successful substance abuse treatment program for 25 years. The board of directors and a committee of staff are working jointly to plan an anniversary celebration. This will also serve the purpose of interpreting to the larger community the available services (possibly recruiting clients) and of getting favorable publicity to launch a new fundraising drive (the agency is expanding). Because there are so many positive outcomes of service delivery, the agency wants to contact all former clients for whom they still have valid addresses to invite them to provide testimony regarding services and to participate in festivities.

4.07a,b; 1.03a; 1.06b; 1.07a,c,k

Commentary

Public relations campaigns highlighting social agencies that provide effective services benefit communities by identifying resources and developing awareness of problems. However, social workers should not engage in solicitation or testimonial endorsement from current clients. Although the agency wants to contact former clients, it could be argued that contacting even former clients with this request would create undue influence on the clients' ability to consent freely. Inevitably, some clients' confidentiality could be compromised, because they may not have made known their former contact with the agency, which could readily, albeit inadvertently, be revealed to other members of a household.

75

A clinical social worker who specializes in treating eating disorders makes regular presentations at PTA meetings, on radio talk shows, and in other venues as an effort at public education. A client whose progress in treatment is noteworthy attributes her increasing well-being to his excellent therapy. The client offered, and the social worker accepted her offer, to appear at some of these interpretive occasions to give hope to those with bulimia, anorexia, obesity, compulsive eating, and other conditions. In return, the social worker reduced the client's treatment fees by half. The pair soon discovered that there are a number of parameters that need to be addressed—for example, whether the client's time in giving testimonials and interpreting treatment is adequately compensated by the 50 percent reduction in fees. As the social worker comments on her progress as an example, does he adequately protect the confidentiality of the details of her "case," its antecedent conditions, family dynamics, and so forth? Is it acceptable for the social worker to measure the "worth" of the arrangement on the basis of new clients recruited from the events at which the client appears?

4.07b; 1.06b,c; 1.07c,d,k; 1.13a,b

Commentary

Even though the client offered to appear at some of these interpretive occasions, it was the clinical social worker's responsibility to evaluate thoroughly the possible consequences and probably to have found means of thanking her and limiting her participation so there was neither the reality or appearance that he had "used her." As a client she is in a vulnerable position, and it is the clinical social worker's responsibility to protect her confidentiality and to foresee the possible harm or exploitation that would ensue or be perceived. Once the fees for her treatment were adjusted on the basis of her appearances, they entered a dual relationship wherein she was an employee. As a clinician, he should strive to avoid a dual relationship, not create one. Fees need to be set on a fair and reasonable basis including consideration of the client's ability to pay. Clinicians should avoid bartering, because these arrangements create the potential for conflict of interests, exploitation, and blurred professional boundaries.

76

Social work doctoral students at a well-known university regularly publish their first articles listed as second authors, using their doctoral committee chairs as the first authors. The school and students accept this as common practice, noting that the committee chairs regularly put great effort into the students' work, help pave the way for publication, and deserve recognition for these efforts. A few of the students have learned that this is not common practice at all schools of social work.

4.08a,b; 5.01b,d

Commentary

The published articles appear to be primarily based on the dissertation research of the students. There is a conflict between the right of the student to authorship and the right of the faculty member to credit for a contribution to the dissertation research. It is customary in some schools of social work and in some schools of related professions for faculty to be second authors on articles related to students' dissertations they directed. Some faculty will claim first or second authorship on articles or research in instances in which they have provided directorship or significant assistance. Some schools of social work consider this misrepresentation. They claim that doctoral research is the work of the student and that, in the role of director, the faculty member has an obligation to contribute his or her knowledge to the project. Some programs might add that not only is this the duty of the director, but also that the director is being paid for this work as part of the faculty role. The *Code of Ethics* states that social workers should take responsibility and credit, including authorship credit, only for work they have performed or to which they have contributed. The burden then is on a school to set policy that protects the rights of the students and rewards the integrity of the faculty member. Social workers should uphold and advance the values and ethics of the profession. Professional integrity requires honesty and, in this case, requires that students not be exploited.

5. Social Workers' Ethical Responsibilities to the Social Work Profession

77

A geriatric social worker has been employed by a for-profit nursing home. Her job requires that she interview and assess new residents, advise them of their rights as clients and residents, and meet at least once per week with each to monitor their progress and help them gain access to needed services. Over time, the social worker began to suspect that the nursing home was not complying with a nursing home reform act and was, in fact, violating client's rights, especially in terms of access to treatment and use of client funds. The social worker discussed her concerns with her supervisor, who suggested that although such things might have occurred, they were aberrations and not regular practice. The social worker continued to gather information regarding residents' complaints and eventually reported her concerns to the local Medicaid office. Soon after her report, the nursing home received word that they would be audited within one week. Immediately after the agency received notification of the audit, the social worker was laid off from the nursing home by its director, who indicated that the facility was having financial difficulties and that he intends to fill her position with a less costly staff person who was also less qualified.

5.01a,b,e; 3.07d; 3.09b,c,d

Commentary

Social work practitioners have an ethical obligation to promote high standards of practice and uphold the values of the profession. It appears that the social worker has a valid ethics concern and is attempting to assume her ethical obligation in correcting abuses. On the other hand, has she made the administrators of her organization aware of her ethical and relevant legal obligations? If the supervisor is a social worker, has she framed her concerns in terms of the obligations that both of them carry as members of the profession? In this situation, did the social worker go through all the channels available through the organization to correct the abuses before she reported to a primary source of authority? The social worker could build a coalition of other professionals within the organization who have similar concerns. It is important for social workers, when confronted with such serious abuses, to seek consultation and to take appropriate action. Because it appears that, as a result of the social worker's advocacy, the employing organization retaliated by terminating her employment, she could initiate a grievance process within the organization, report to a personnel committee of a board, or seek legal action. If there is no mechanism available within the organization, the peer review process of NASW could be considered as a means of negotiating some changes in the agency's policies and in attempting to resolve her conflict with the nursing home facility.

78

While researching practice methods related to his client population—children with emotional disturbance—a clinical social worker in a residential treatment setting learned of a controversial intervention in which the therapist physically holds a child for a period of time. He reviewed professional literature claiming that the practice appears to have been effective treatment for some children with severe attachment and behavior disorders. He also found social work articles that were extremely critical of the method, calling it coercive, counterproductive, and injurious to children's mental health. Interested in gaining more information, the social worker attended a week-long training session regarding the method. He concludes that one of his clients is the sort of child for whom this treatment seems appropriate.

5.02c; 1.03a,c; 1.04b,c; 1.10; 4.01b,c

Commentary

The social worker seems to have covered many areas in his consideration of using a new intervention. He has reviewed the literature both pro and con and has attended a week-long training session (continuing education) to give himself greater familiarity. If he now consults with the child's parents or guardians and gives them the information he has, he can seek their permission and provide them with an informed consent statement to sign. He must be certain to include in his statement the possible risk or harm that the child might experience.

Subject Index

NOTE: *All entries refer to vignette numbers, not page numbers.*

Acknowledging credit, 76
Administration, 20, 37, 54, 66, 67, 70, 77
Adolescent clients
 privacy/confidentiality issues and, 7, 32, 40
 sexual orientation of, 54
Adoption, by social worker, 16
AIDS/HIV, 26, 40, 43, 54

Barter arrangements, 52
Billing, 27, 42, 53, 65

Child abuse, 45
Child placement, 6. *See also* Foster placement
Client records, 7, 27, 31, 42, 47
Clients
 adolescent, 7, 32, 40, 54
 commitment to, 1–6, 16, 25, 26, 32, 49, 65, 69
 deceased, 36
 sexual relationships with, 8, 28, 48–50, 59
 who lack decision-making capacity, 6, 7, 9, 17, 25
Collaboration, between disciplines, 12
Colleagues
 impairment of, 64
 sexual relationships with, 58
 unethical conduct of, 8, 11, 59–60
Commitment
 to clients, 1–6, 16, 25, 26, 32, 49, 65, 69
 to employers, 2, 3, 10, 14, 34, 37, 45, 47, 53–54, 56, 66, 68, 70–71, 77
Competence
 social, 2, 4, 6, 10–12, 30, 37
 of social workers, 10, 21, 58, 67, 78
Confidentiality, 1, 3, 27, 28, 31, 34–36, 38, 47, 56, 60, 68–69, 74, 75
 See also Privacy
 adolescent clients and, 7, 32
 breach of, 43
 child abuse and, 45
 child welfare and, 39
 client records and, 47
 client's right to, 8, 22, 75
 criminal suspects and, 42
 duty to protect and, 40
 office practices and, 33
 safety issues and, 41
 in small communities, 30
 social worker's right to protection and, 44
 subpoenas and, 36, 46
 translators and, 37
Conflicts of interest
 adoption child of client as, 16
 in dual and multiple relationships, 5, 14–16, 20, 24, 25, 27–29, 50, 58, 61
 power of attorney and, 17, 26
 preferential treatment and, 18
 related to business interests, 13, 15, 19, 21, 22
 responsibilities in order to avoid, 5, 23, 34, 35, 38, 46, 48, 50, 52, 57, 59, 66, 68, 74–75
 sexual relationships and, 49
 sexual relationships with colleagues as, 58
Consultation, 5, 8, 12, 26, 29, 31, 39–41, 43, 44, 48, 50, 58, 61, 63, 67
Controversial interventions, 78
Credit, for work performed, 76
Criminal evidence, 42
Cultural competence, 2, 4, 6, 10–12, 30, 37

Cultural factors
  community supports and, 30
  confidentiality and translators and, 38
  foster placement and, 4
  physical abuse and, 2
  professionals as interpreters and, 12
  treatment programs and, 10

Deception, 27, 53, 65, 69, 72, 73
Decision-making capacity, 6, 7, 9, 17, 25
Depression, 73
Discrimination, 37
  based on fiscal reimbursement, 66
  foster placement and, 4
  racial, 70
  in selection of transplant candidates, 71
  sexual orientation and, 6, 54, 69
  welfare recipients and, 3
Dishonesty, 27, 53, 65, 69, 72, 73
Dissertation research, 76
Divorce, 46

Eating disorders, 75
Education, 62, 63
Evaluation
  ethical considerations in, 10, 71, 78
  performance, 64

Foster placement, 4, 69
Fraud, 27, 53, 65, 69, 72, 73

Gifts, to social workers, 26

HIV. *See* AIDS/HIV
Homeless individuals, 9

Impairment
  of colleagues, 64
  of social workers, 73
Informed consent
  client protection and, 35
  for evaluation and research participants, 10, 71, 78
  responsibilities related to, 1, 6, 8–9, 12, 14, 17, 30, 32, 34, 37, 63, 74
Intake interviews, 31
Integrity of the profession, 6, 11, 38, 59, 66, 76–77
Interruption of services, 2, 57

Job performance, 64

Lesbian relationships
  child placement and, 6, 69
  following termination of services, 28

Medical power of attorney, 17, 26
Mental health counseling, 11
Misrepresentation, 6, 73

Native Americans, 4, 10
Nursing homes, 77

Organ transplants, 71

Paraprofessionals, 11
Payment for services, 52, 53, 75
Performance evaluation, 64
Physical abuse, 2
Physical contact, 78
Political action, 3, 9–11, 18, 29–30, 47, 54, 55, 65, 66, 69–72
Posttermination contracts, 23
Power of attorney, 17, 26
Pregnancy, adolescent, 7
Privacy, 1, 3, 8, 27, 28, 30, 34–46, 56, 60, 68–69, 74–75. *See also* Confidentiality
  adolescent clients and, 7, 32
  client records and, 47
  client's right to, 22
  MSW students and, 31
  office practices and, 33
  subpoenas and, 36, 46
Pro bono service, 55
Public participation, 29
Public relations campaigns, 74
Publishing, 76

Racial discrimination, 70
Records. *See* Client records
Referral for services, 2, 5, 14, 48, 67, 71
Religious communities, 62
Research, 10, 71, 78
Responsibilities to society, 1

Self-determination, 1, 3, 9, 14, 17, 20, 32, 68
  adolescent clients and, 7
  child placement and, 6
  client's right to, 8
Services
  ethical issues in billing for, 53
  interruption of, 2, 57
  payment for, 52, 53, 75
  pro bono, 55
  referral for, 2, 5, 14, 48, 67
  termination of, 5, 14, 23, 28, 54, 56, 57
Sexual abuse, 1, 39, 60
Sexual orientation, 6, 54, 69
Sexual relationships
  with clients, 8, 28, 48–50, 59
  with colleagues, 58
  prior client–social worker, 51
Social action, 3, 9–11, 18, 29–30, 47, 54, 55, 65, 66, 69–72
Social diversity, 2, 4, 6, 10–12, 30, 37
Social welfare, 6, 25, 39, 72

Social workers
  adopting child of client by, 16
  concerns for safety of, 25
  controversial interventions by, 78
  in dual and multiple relationships, 5
  gifts to, 26
  mental health of, 73
Solicitations, 74, 75
Stalking, 44
Subpoenas, 36, 46
Substance abuse treatment, 10, 41, 74
Suicide/suicide ideation, 36, 67
Supervision, 58, 61, 63

Termination of services, 5, 14, 54, 55
  employee termination and, 56
  relationships with clients following, 23, 28
  stalking following, 44
  transfer or referral and, 57
Training, 62, 63
Translators, 37
Transplant candidates, 71

Unethical conduct of colleagues, 8, 11, 59, 60

Welfare recipients, 3

Section Index

NOTE: *All entries refer to vignette numbers, not page numbers.*

1.01, 1, 2, 3, 4, 5, 6, 16, 25, 26, 32, 49, 65, 69
1.02, 1, 3, 6, 7, 8, 9, 14, 17, 20, 32, 68
1.03a, 1, 8, 9, 14, 17, 30, 32, 34, 35, 37, 63, 74, 78
1.03b, 12, 30, 37
1.03c, 6, 9, 12, 35, 78
1.03d, 9
1.03f, 34, 35
1.04a, 67
1.04b, 10, 78
1.04c, 10, 21, 78
1.05, 2, 10, 11, 37
1.05a, 12
1.05b, 4, 6, 12, 30
1.05c, 4, 6
1.06a, 13, 14, 15, 16, 17, 18, 49, 50, 61, 66
1.06b, 5, 13, 14, 19, 20, 21, 22, 34, 35, 49, 50, 52, 57, 74, 75
1.06c, 5, 15, 16, 17, 18, 21, 23, 24, 25, 26, 27, 28, 29, 38, 48, 49, 50, 52, 59, 75
1.06d, 46, 49, 68
1.07a, 3, 7, 22, 27, 30, 31, 32, 33, 34, 69, 74
1.07b, 3, 7, 35, 36, 68
1.07c, 1, 3, 7, 8, 32, 33, 35, 36, 37, 38, 39, 40, 41, 42, 43, 44, 45, 60, 68, 69, 74, 75
1.07d, 1, 7, 32, 33, 35, 37, 40, 41, 42, 43, 46, 47, 75
1.07e, 1, 7, 33, 40, 41, 42, 44, 45, 46, 47
1.07f, 46
1.07g, 46
1.07h, 47
1.07i, 34
1.07j, 36, 46
1.07k, 34, 35, 74, 75
1.07l, 42
1.07n, 56
1.07q, 43, 45
1.07r, 28, 36
1.09a, 8, 48, 49, 59
1.09b, 49
1.09c, 49, 50
1.09d, 51
1.10, 78
1.13a, 52, 75
1.13b, 52, 75
1.13c, 53
1.14, 6, 7, 9, 17, 25
1.15, 2, 57
1.16b, 54, 55, 56
1.16d, 5, 20
1.16e, 14, 55, 56, 57
1.16f, 14, 56

2.05, 12
2.05a, 5, 8, 26, 29, 31, 39, 40, 41, 43, 44, 48, 50, 67
2.05c, 31, 48, 50
2.06a, 2, 5, 14, 48, 67
2.07a, 58
2.09a, 64
2.09b, 64
2.11a, 59, 60
2.11b, 8, 59, 60
2.11c, 8, 59, 60
2.11d, 8, 59, 60
2.11e, 11

3.01c, 58, 61, 63
3.02a, 62
3.02d, 62, 63
3.03, 64
3.04a, 27, 31
3.04b, 7
3.04c, 7, 31, 42
3.05, 27, 65

3.07a, 20, 37
3.07b, 66, 70
3.07c, 67
3.07d, 54, 66, 70, 77
3.09a, 3, 47, 56, 70
3.09b, 2, 37, 56, 66, 70, 71, 77
3.09c, 10, 14, 34, 37, 45, 47, 54, 56, 66, 70, 71, 77
3.09d, 14, 34, 37, 45, 47, 53, 54, 56, 66, 68, 70, 71, 77

4.01a, 58
4.01b, 78
4.01c, 10, 78
4.02, 3, 4, 6, 37, 54, 69, 70, 71
4.04, 27, 53, 65, 69, 72, 73
4.05a, 73
4.05b, 73
4.06a, 6
4.07a, 74
4.07b, 74, 75

4.08a, 76
4.08b, 76

5.01a, 59, 66, 77
5.01b, 6, 76, 77
5.01c, 38
5.01d, 76
5.01e, 11, 77
5.02a, 71
5.02c, 10, 78

6.01, 6, 25, 39, 72
6.02, 29
6.04, 29
6.04a, 3, 9, 11, 47, 55, 65, 69, 70, 71, 72
6.04b, 3, 9, 10, 18, 30, 54, 66, 69, 70, 71, 72
6.04c, 3, 10, 30, 70
6.04d, 3, 70

Send Us Your Ethics Dilemma

Current Controversies in Social Work Ethics will be updated annually. You could be one of the contributors!

Send us your ethics quandary or problem, regardless of how you resolved it, and it will be considered for publication. If we accept your submission, we will edit it and send it to all subscribers. You will not be identified or credited as the submitter if your dilemma is used; your submission will be acknowledged in writing.

This handbook is intended to be interactive. We welcome any comments.

You may photocopy this form.

---

1. Write a brief (one or two paragraphs) vignette of your ethics dilemma, **altering all identifying information to absolutely protect all people and agencies involved.** Use a separate sheet if necessary.

_____
_____
_____
_____
_____
_____
_____
_____
_____
_____
_____
_____
_____
_____
_____
_____
_____
_____

Continued

2. Write a brief commentary (one or two paragraphs) on your vignette to include
   - the conflict of values or priorities
   - the unresolved problem
   - a list of the *Code of Ethics* standards that are relevant and should be applied in resolving the dilemma, listing the most relevant standard first. Use a separate sheet if necessary.

   _____
   _____
   _____
   _____
   _____
   _____
   _____
   _____
   _____
   _____
   _____
   _____

3. Send your submission to
   Manager, Office of Ethics and Adjudication
   National Association of Social Workers
   750 First Street, NE, Suite 700
   Washington, DC 20002-4241
   1-800-638-8799
   Fax: 202-336-8327

4. Yes, please put my name on your list to receive information about the annual updates to *Current Controversies in Social Work Ethics*.

   Name _____

   Address _____

   _____

   City _____ State _____ Zip _____

   Daytime Phone _____

   Fax _____ E-mail _____

   ❏ I am   ❏ am not a member of NASW.

RISK MANAGEMENT STRATEGIES TO HELP YOU MINIMIZE EXPOSURE TO MALPRACTICE LITIGATION!

Current Controversies in Social Work Ethics: Case Examples, *by NASW Code of Ethics Revision Committee, Frederic Reamer, Chairperson.* Presents a cross-section of real examples of ethics dilemmas faced by social workers in contemporary practice situations. A companion work to the *NASW Code of Ethics,* this practical and thought-provoking handbook offers commentaries on related considerations and implications that help the reader untangle the controversies and competing values associated with ethical decision making.

6" x 9" pamphlet. Item #3002. 100 pages. 1998. $8.50

Professional Choices: Ethics at Work. This educational videotape presents interviews with a number of social work practitioners, educators, and administrators as they discuss ethical social work practice. Each segment covers frequently encountered ethics issues related to confidentiality, boundary issues, indiscretion, and client self-determination.

Videotape. Item #V2. 40 minutes. VHS 1/2". $65.00

NASW Code of Ethics. The *NASW Code of Ethics* is a set of standards for the professional conduct of social workers. The 1996 *Code* is imperative for use in schools and in-service training for agencies. It includes four sections: mission and values of the profession, purpose of the code, ethical principles, and ethical standards.

Pamphlet. Item #X2A. $60/100

Ethical Standards in Social Work: A Critical Review of the *NASW Code of Ethics*, *by Frederic G. Reamer.* Here is the first comprehensive, in-depth examination of the code of ethics of the social work profession. With this practical guide, which includes many case examples, you'll have a firm foundation for making ethical decisions and minimizing malpractice and liability risk.

ISBN: 0-87101-293-6. 1998. Item #2936. $24.95

Prudent Practice: A Guide for Managing Malpractice Risk, *by Mary Kay Houston-Vega and Elane M. Nuehring with Elisabeth R. Daguio.* Social workers and other human services professionals face a heightened risk of malpractice suits in today's litigious society. The NASW Press offers practitioners a complete practice guide to increasing competence and managing the risk of malpractice. Included in the book and on disk are 25 sample forms and 5 sample fact sheets to distribute to clients.

ISBN: 0-87101-267-7. 1997. Item #2677. $42.95

(Order form on reverse side)

ORDER FORM

	Title	Item #	Price	Total
__	Current Controversies on Social Work Ethics	3002	$8.50	_____
__	Professional Choices	V2	$65.00	_____
__	NASW Code of Ethics *(per 100 pamphlets)*	X2A	$60.00	_____
__	Ethical Standards in Social Work	2936	$24.95	_____
__	Prudent Practice (Word for Windows disk)	2677	$42.95	_____
__	Prudent Practice (Macintosh disk)	2677A	$42.95	_____
			Subtotal	_____
		+ 10% postage and handling		_____
			Total	_____

❒ I've enclosed my check or money order for $ _____.

❒ Please charge my   ❒ NASW Visa*   ❒ Other Visa   ❒ MasterCard

_____   _____
Credit Card Number   Expiration Date

Signature _____

Use of this card generates funds in support of the social work profession.

Name _____

Address _____

City _____ State/Province _____

Country _____ Zip _____

Phone _____ E-mail _____

NASW Member # (if applicable) _____

(Please make checks payable to NASW Press. Prices are subject to change.)

NASW PRESS
P. O. Box 431
Annapolis JCT, MD 20701
USA

Credit card orders call
1-800-227-3590
(In the Metro Wash., DC, area, call 301-317-8688)
Or fax your order to 301-206-7989
Or order online at http://www.naswpress.org

Visit our Web site at http://www.naswpress.org.

The primary mission of the social work profession is to enhance human well-being and help meet the basic human needs of all people, with particular attention to the needs and empowerment of people who are vulnerable, oppressed, and living in poverty. A historic and defining feature of social work is the profession's focus on individual well-being in a social context and the well-being of society. Fundamental to social work is attention to the environmental forces that create, contribute to, and address problems in living.

National Association of Social Workers
750 First Street, NE, Suite 700
Washington, DC 20002-4241
1-800-638-8799
http://www.socialworkers.org

ISBN 0-87101-300-2

50850>

9 780871 013002